The Pioneer Burial

A high-status Anglian warrior burial from Wollaston Northamptonshire

Ian Meadows

With contributions by

Rob Atkins, Alison Draper, J N James, Lloyd Laing, Matthew Ponting,
Anthony Read, Jenny Wakely, Penelope Walton-Rogers,
and Jacqui Watson

Illustrations by

Olly Dindol, Jacqueline Harding and James Ladocha

Archaeopress Archaeology

Archaeopress Publishing Ltd
Summertown Pavilion
18-24 Middle Way
Summertown
Oxford OX2 7LG

www.archaeopress.com

ISBN 978-1-78969-119-1
ISBN 978-1-78969-120-7 (e-Pdf)

© Archaeopress and the individual authors 2019

Cover: The conserved helmet
Back cover: Artist's impression of the Pioneer helmet

All rights reserved. No part of this book may be reproduced, or transmitted, in any form or by any means, electronic, mechanical, photocopying or otherwise, without the prior written permission of the copyright owners.

This book is available direct from Archaeopress or from our website www.archaeopress.com

Contents

List of Figures iii

Contributors v

Acknowledgements vii

Chapter 1 Introduction 1
    Project background 1
    Archaeological background.. 4
    Topography and geology 7

Chapter 2 Excavation 9
    Burial location 9
    The excavation methodology 9
    The grave 9
    The grave goods 11

Chapter 3 Artefacts.. 17
    Overview 17
    The helmet *by Ian Meadows* 17
        The brow band 17
        Nose to nape band 17
        Lateral bands 24
        External reinforcing ribs 24
        The infill plates 25
        The cheek guards 25
        The eyebrows and nasal 26
        The Boar crest 26
        The helmet in the grave 26
    Conservation report on the helmet *by Anthony Read* 26
    Organic material associated with the helmet *by Jacqui Watson* 31
    Hanging bowl *by Lloyd Laing* 32
    Analysis of the hanging bowl *by Matthew Ponting* 33
        Scientific examination 33
        Microscopic examination 33
        Chemical analysis 34
        Discussion 34
    The sword *by Ian Meadows* 36
    Organic material associated with the sword *by Jacqui Watson* 36
        Scabbard 36
    Other artefacts.. 38
    The knife, buckles, iron rods and clothing hook *by Ian Meadows* 38
        The knife... 38
        The buckles 38
            Buckle A (RA2) 38
            Buckle C (RA3) 38
            Buckle B (RA1) 39
         The iron rods 39
         The clothing hook.. 39
    Conservation report on the buckles *by Alison Draper* 39
        Introduction 39
        Condition.. 39
        Treatment 39
        Descriptions 39
            RA3, buckle C 39
            RA2, buckle A 41
            RA1, buckle B 41

RA1, side 2	41
RA4, described as miscellaneous fragments	41
RA4, A-F	41
RA4	41
RA5, described as plough deposits	42
RA5, individual fragments B-D (Fig 3.33).	42
Textiles remains possibly relating to bedding *by Penelope Walton-Rogers*	43
Introduction	43
Textile A	43
Textile B	43
Conclusion	45

Chapter 4 Human remains 47

Skeletal report *by Jenny Wakely with note on dental remains by J N James*	47
The skull	47
The legs	47
The dentition	47
Summary	47

Chapter 5 Discussion *by Rob Atkins and Ian Meadows* 49

Overview	49
The location of the Pioneer burial	49
Routeways in relation to the Pioneer burial	49
The River Nene and land boundaries	53
Burial time period	53
Wollaston in relation to Saxon administrative organisation	54
Nature of the grave	56
Barrow mound	56
The grave	57
Importance of the burial	58
Helmet	58
Hanging bowl	61
Pattern-welded sword	61
Pioneer burial and 'Christianity'	62
Contemporary probable Christian burial comparisons	63
Conclusions	64

Bibliography 65

List of Figures

Figure 1.1. Location and sites in Northamptonshire mentioned in the text...1
Figure 1.2. The site and its environs with Roman road and cropmarks located 2
Figure 1.3. Areas to be excavated and protected areas within the site with Pioneer burial location recorded (after Kidd 1995) 3
Figure 1.4. Daily Mail article dated 23 April 1997 5
Figure 1.5. Article in Northampton Chronicle and Echo dated 23 April 1997 6
Figure 1.6. Helmet restored with Ian Meadows directly behind talking to colleagues (Greg Phillips, Graham Cadman, Vikki Pearson, Martin Ellison, Ian Meadows, Rob Atkins, Glenn Foard, Brenda Perryman, Jenny Ballinger and Ann Bond) 7

Figure 2.1. Plan of burial showing grave goods 10
Figure 2.2. view of the burial, looking south 11
Figure 2.3. Vertical view of sword, femurs and part of helmet 11
Figure 2.4. Remains of the skull, looking south 12
Figure 2.5. Hanging bowl, skull and cobble, looking south-west...12
Figure 2.6. Detail of sword grip and knife 13
Figure 2.7. Helmet from above 14
Figure 2.8. Helmet in ground from side 14
Figure 2.9. Helmet in cling film 15
Figure 2.10. Plaster being applied to helmet 15
Figure 2.11. Machine excavation trenches around the burial, looking north-west 15

Figure 3.1. The helmet, front 18
Figure 3.2. The helmet, right side, largely showing interior of left side 19
Figure 3.3. The helmet, rear 20
Figure 3.4. The helmet, left side 21
Figure 3.5. The conserved helmet 22
Figure 3.6. Views of the helmet following conservation 23
Figure 3.7. The helmet and its component parts 24
Figure 3.8. Helmet details 25
Figure 3.9. Helmet being X-rayed 26
Figure 3.10. X-ray of helmet 27
Figure 3.11. Helmet being cleaned 27
Figure 3.12. Interior of cheek guard after cleaning with pupae casts around central rivet 28
Figure 3.13. Nick Gore and George Jeavons inspect the helmet in Leicester 29
Figure 3.14. Unconserved boar crest 29
Figure 3.15. Detail of boar crest after cleaning 29
Figure 3.16. Helmet in CT scanner 30
Figure 3.17. Results examined on computer 30
Figure 3.18. Hanging bowl 32
Figure 3.19. The sword 37
Figure 3.20. The knife, buckles and clothing hook 38
Figure 3.21. X-radiograph of RA3 (buckle C) 40
Figure 3.22. RA3 (buckle C), textile seen to left of black line 40

Figure 3.23. RA3 (buckle C), other side, semi-circular piece of metal can be seen 40
Figure 3.24. X-radiograph of RA2 (buckle A) 40
Figure 3.25. RA2 (buckle A), after cleaning, side 1 40
Figure 3.26. RA2 (buckle A), after cleaning, side 2 40
Figure 3.27. X-radiograph of RA1 (buckle B) 41
Figure 3.28. RA1 (buckle B), side 1 41
Figure 3.29. RA1 (buckle B), side 2 41
Figure 3.30. RA4 41
Figure 3.31. RA5 A, X-radiograph of soil block 42
Figure 3.32. RA5 Group A from soil block (side with circular feature) 42
Figure 3.33. RA5, individual fragments B-E 43
Figure 3.34. Detail of textiles 43
Figure 3.35. Textiles 44

Figure 5.1. Helmet, hanging bowl and pattern-welded sword 50
Figure 5.2. Pioneer burial in its national setting with other Saxon (and Viking) helmets located 51
Figure 5.3. View along the line of the Roman road to the Pioneer burial, looking south-west 52
Figure 5.4. Artist's impression of the Pioneer helmet 59

Contributors

Rob Atkins
Reporting and publications manager, MOLA

Alison Draper
Conservator, Manchester Metropolitan University

J N James
Lecturer in Dentistry, Leicester University

Lloyd Laing
Associate Professor, Nottingham University

Ian Meadows
Former Senior Project Manager, MOLA

Matthew Ponting
Senior Lecturer in Archaeology, Classics and Egyptology, University of Liverpool

Anthony Read
Head of Collections and Learning, National Museum of Ireland, Dublin

Jenny Wakely
Former Lecturer at School of Medicine, University of Leicester (deceased)

Penelope Walton-Rogers
Freelance textile specialist, The Anglo-Saxon Laboratory

Jacqui Watson
Organic material specialist at Ancient Monuments Laboratory, English Heritage

Acknowledgements

MOLA (Museum of London Archaeology) formerly Northamptonshire Archaeology would like to thank the two then land owners, Peter Gammage and the late John Minney. The staff of Hanson UK (and previously Pioneer Aggregates) was closely involved throughout the work including Brian Chapman, Roy Clarke and Mark Page, Land and Planning Manager, and Nick Gore and George Jeavons who organised the funding for the excavation stage. Mark Page kindly arranged funding for this publication on the Pioneer burial and for the forthcoming publication on the Wollaston excavation sites. The boar-crested helmet found was termed the "Pioneer Helmet" after Pioneer Aggregates UK who fully funded the conservation, and the cost of the excavations.

Many specialists advised throughout the process of conservation and analysis including Professor R Cramp, Dominic Tweddle, Leslie Webster, Betty Coatsworth, Professor J Hines and Antony Reed. The staff of the Royal Armouries Museum in Leeds also provided support and advice in particular for the helmet. Janet Lang of the British Museum carried out the specialist X-ray examination of the sword. Nottingham University carried out analysis of the hanging bowl and the millefiori.

The original archaeological work was monitored by Sandy Kidd and Glenn Foard at Northamptonshire County Council. Ian Meadows was the project manager for Northamptonshire Archaeology with the fieldwork on the Pioneer burial carried out by Rob Atkins, Chris Jones and Joe Prentice. Steve Critchley metal detected the site and found the burial. Charlotte Walker of Northamptonshire HER kindly provided copious amounts of data through a search on Saxon burials, hanging bowls and swords recovered in the county. Chris Fern and Jenni Butterworth supplied information on the Staffordshire Hoard helmet fragments. Stephen Young and CLASP kindly provided details of the burials, including the sword burial, found during excavations at Whitehall Farm, Nether Heyford, Northamptonshire. Dr Chris Caple helpfully sent his *Medieval Archaeology* submission on the Yarm helmet which was especially useful. Daily Mail (Solo Syndication) and Northampton Chronicle and Echo have kindly allowed reproduction of their articles.

The Pioneer burial artefacts have been kept together and are on long term display at the Royal Armouries, Leeds.

Rob Atkins edited the client report (Meadows 2004) to publication. Proof reading has been carried out by Andy Chapman, Mark Holmes, Ian Meadows and Stephen Parry.

Chapter 1

Introduction

Project background

MOLA (Museum of London Archaeology) formerly Northamptonshire Archaeology carried out excavations on behalf of Pioneer Aggregates UK, now part of Hanson UK at Wollaston Quarry, Northamptonshire. The site (Figs 1.1 and 1.2) lies 2km to the west of the small town of Wollaston just above a wide floodplain to the east of the River Nene. The area was known for the quality of the crop marks produced by the gravel soils that had been recorded by aerial photography and archaeological excavations have occurred there for many years in advance of gravel extraction by various aggregate companies (RCHM 1979).

An archaeological evaluation in 1990 for Pioneer Aggregates took place between c1km to 2.5km to the north-east of the Pioneer helmet site on land to the north of Hardwater Road and comprised 122 trial trenches within eight fields (Fig 1.1; Jackson nd; Jackson 1991). This area was subsequently excavated between 1993 and 1996 and produced clusters of Neolithic pits. The entire

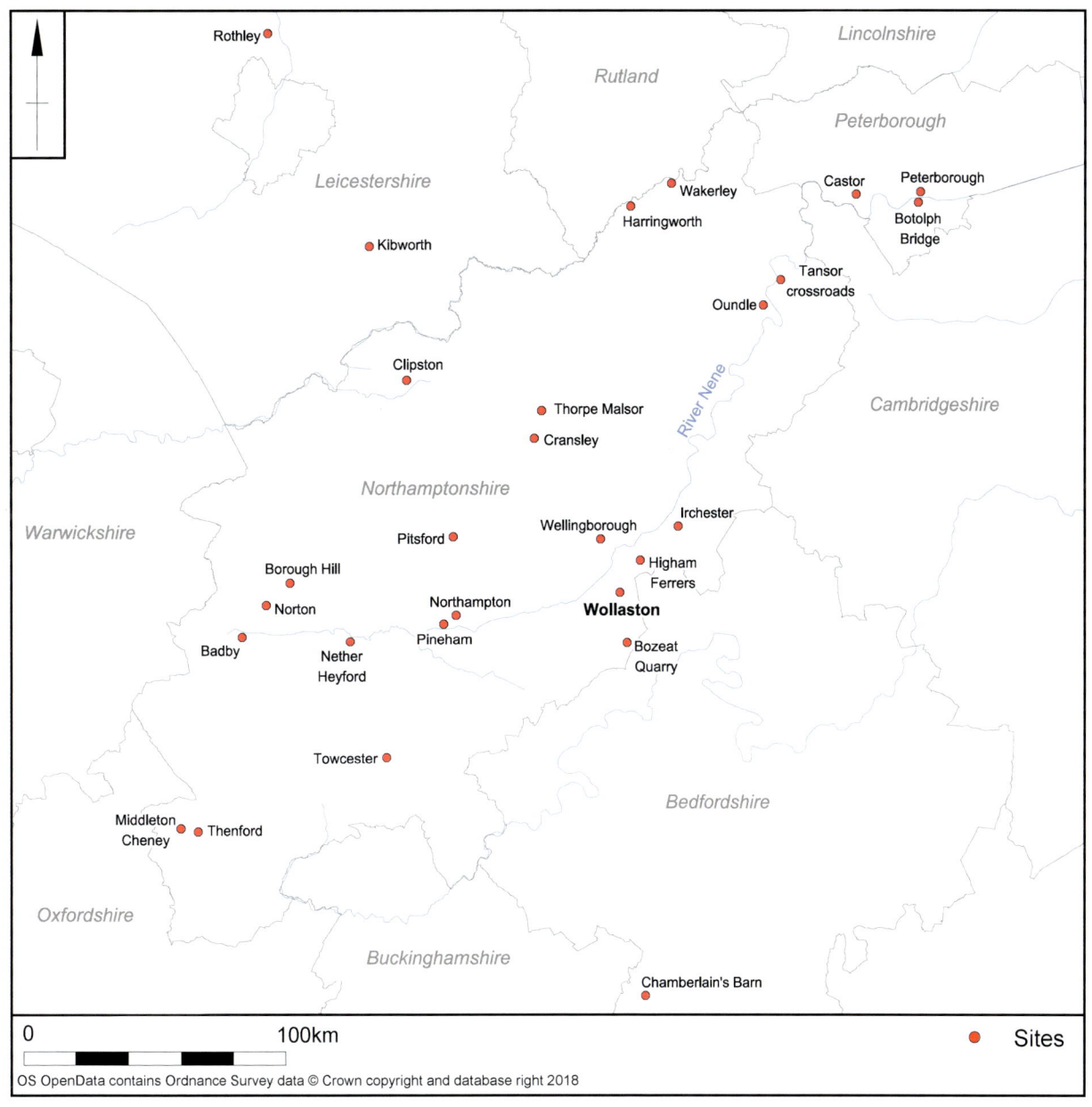

FIGURE 1.1. LOCATION AND SITES IN NORTHAMPTONSHIRE MENTIONED IN THE TEXT

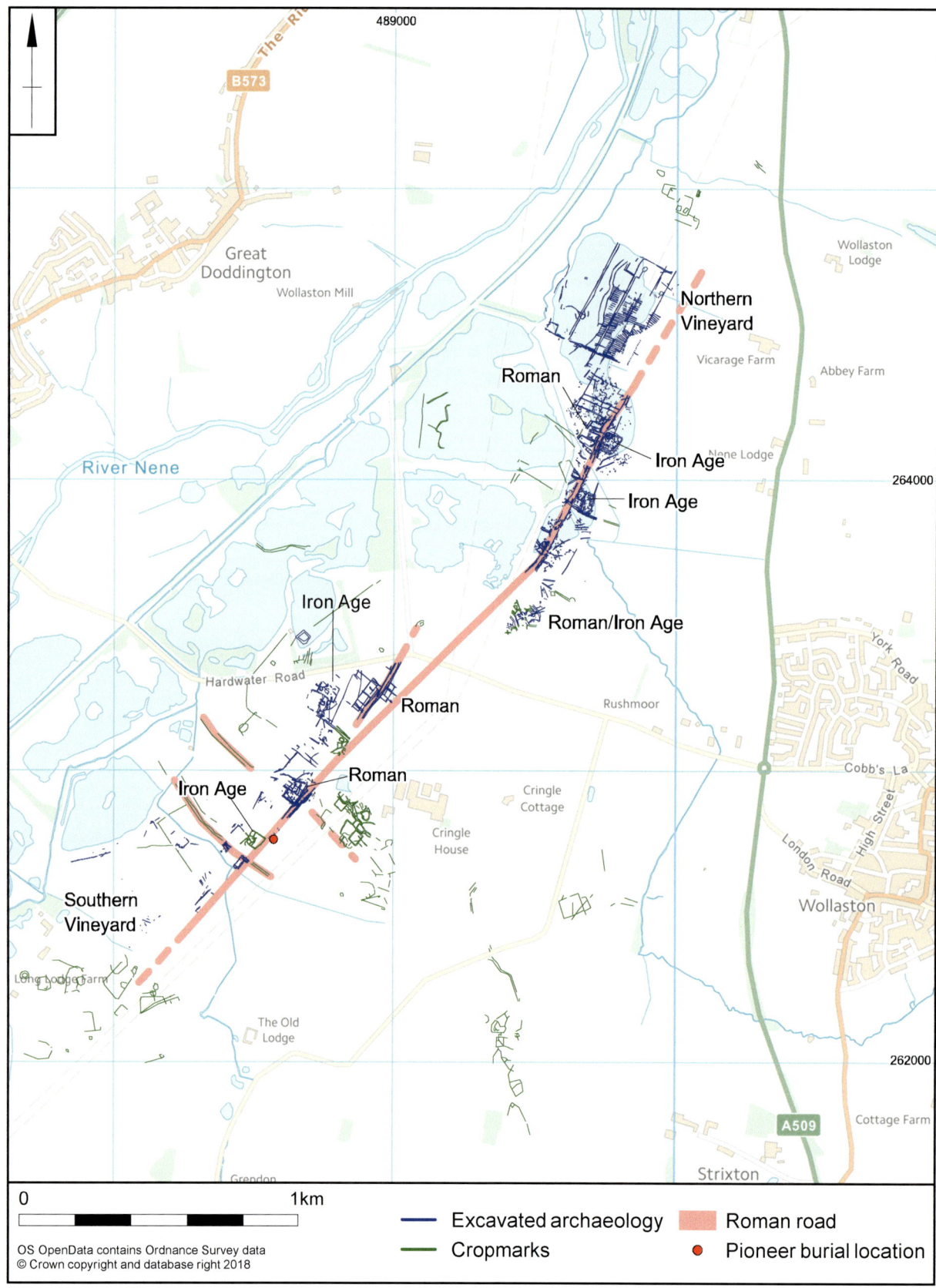

Figure 1.2. The site and its environs with Roman road and cropmarks located

landscape was divided up by an extensive system of pit alignments in the late Bronze Age/early Iron Age. It was subsequently occupied by Iron Age to Roman farmsteads in a linear alignment north-east to south-west along an Iron Age droveway that developed into a Roman road (Meadows 1994; Meadows and Atkins forthcoming; Fig

1.2). At the northern end of the quarry the first proven Roman vineyard from Roman Britain was discovered, comprising an extensive system of pastinatio trenches some of which were found to contain vitis pollen (Brown *et al* 2001).

Pioneer Aggregates decided to extend their quarry within land to the south-west of this original area and submitted a Planning Application (WP/94/439c) on land to the south of Hardwater Road. It was within this area where the Pioneer helmet was subsequently found. On the advice of Northamptonshire Heritage, an archaeological evaluation was undertaken prior to the determination of the planning application. The work conformed to an archaeological brief by Northamptonshire Heritage (Kidd 1994).

The new area comprised *c*71ha of arable land within the floodplain of the River Nene and an archaeological evaluation was carried out in two stages (Meadows 1995; Parry and Audouy 1995). The archaeological work found extensive activity similar to that found to the north comprising a system of linear boundaries demarked by pit alignments dating to the late Bronze Age/early Iron Age. This formed the basis for a co-axial system of boundaries in the middle and later Iron Age with most of the earlier boundaries continuing to be respected in these later periods. The Iron Age land divisions were perpetuated after the Roman Conquest with, in several instances, Roman farmsteads simply being located adjacent to the Iron Age examples (Meadows 1995; Parry and Audouy 1995; Meadows and Atkins forthcoming).

This landscape was dominated by a significant routeway, which was a continuation of that excavated to the north (above). Its earliest phase had been defined by a pit alignment, which during the middle and later Iron Age became a droveway and following the Roman conquest became a road possibly linking the small towns at Irchester and Towcester. The Iron Age and Roman landscape demonstrated considerable levels of rural conservatism with regards the size and shape of land allotments. No early to middle Saxon remains were found in the evaluations but medieval and post-medieval ridge and furrow cultivation was uncovered.

As a result of the evaluations a recording action brief was provided by Northamptonshire Heritage (Kidd 1995; Fig 1.3). This figure attached to the Brief shows the thought processes after the evaluation stage of both Northamptonshire's Heritage and also the Pioneer Quarry by detailing what areas needed quarrying and thereby how much of the site should be excavated

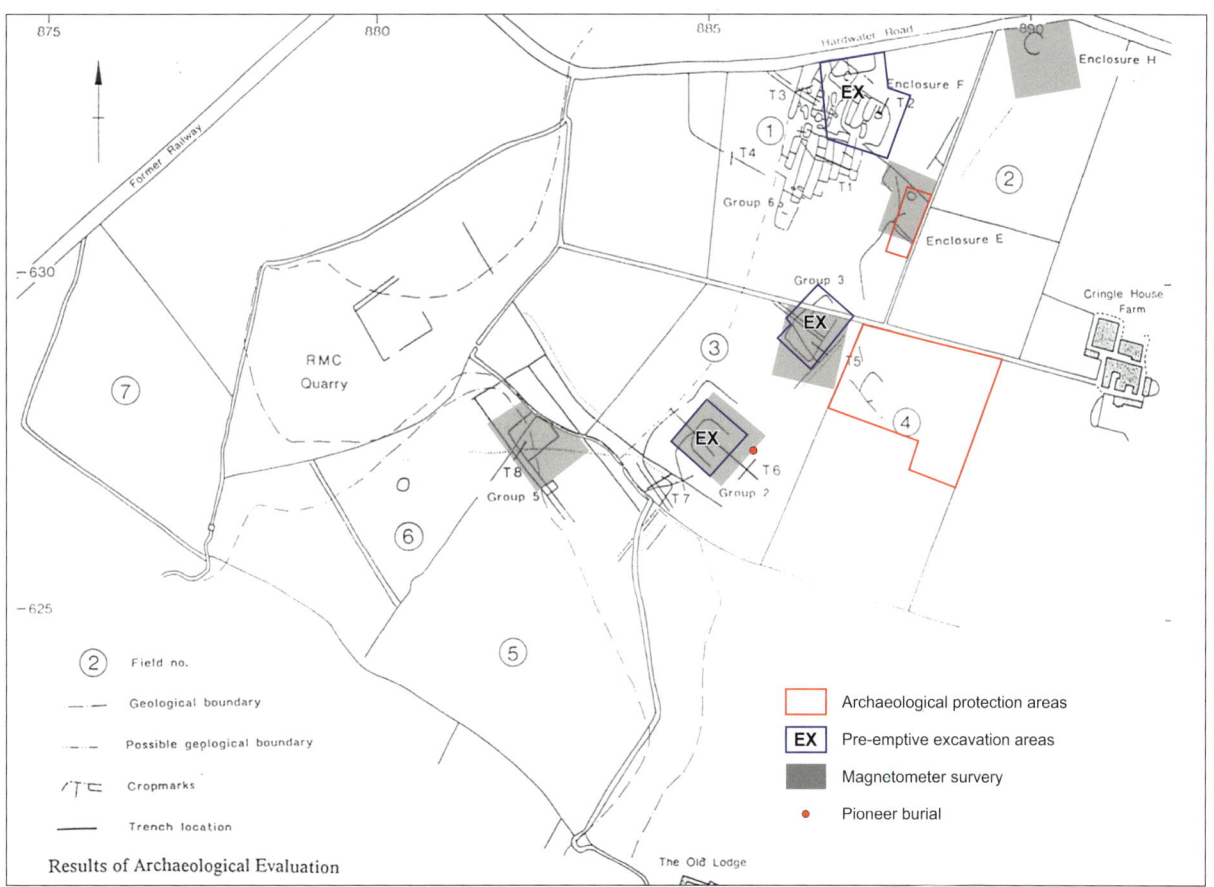

FIGURE 1.3. AREAS TO BE EXCAVATED AND PROTECTED AREAS WITHIN THE SITE WITH PIONEER BURIAL LOCATION RECORDED (AFTER KIDD 1995)

as well as protected areas. This Brief outlined the justification for further investigation, recording and publication of the archaeological remains. The brief stipulated; "pre-emptive excavation of three Iron Age/Roman settlements and a combination of targeted small scale excavation ahead of topsoil stripping, an intensive watching brief during stripping, salvage excavation following stripping and environmental sampling to investigate the coaxial field system and other significant remains."

The areas recorded to be excavated or protected in the Brief (Fig 1.3) was not fixed and was more of an initial plan which changed after rethinking by the Pioneer Quarry on what and where they proposed to extract. The actual archaeological areas excavated are recorded in Figure 1.2. In addition, more geophysical work was undertaken in the quarry than had been originally envisaged (Meadows and Atkins forthcoming).

The Brief stated than an appropriate level of investigation should take place within all parts of the site which were subject to topsoil stripping. It stated that there had to be a watching brief and contingency with 160 person days allocated for salvage recording if any unidentified remains of county or national importance were revealed within the site (Kidd 1995, section 2.5).

During the subsequent archaeological work the Iron Age and Roman settlement sites were excavated and the results showed a considerable continuity of landscape. The farmsteads with their related field systems (as well as the earlier pit alignments) respected the floodplain and were all located at the limit of medieval alluviation perhaps suggesting the extent of the flooding.

Only very limited evidence of post Roman activity was recovered in the main excavation areas, comprising two separate fragments of Saxon brooches (recovered by metal detection) and two small collections of pottery. The pottery was recovered within 500m of the Pioneer burial; one comprised a surface scatter and the other from a small amorphous feature. Because of the paucity of evidence the floodplain was thought to have been marginal in the post-Roman period.

Steve Critchley routinely carried out systematic metal detector surveying throughout the project across all the excavation and topsoil stripped areas. As the area had been farmed for many years ferrous signals were not generally investigated as they proved to be mostly horseshoes, undiagnostic nails or other modern detritus. However, in March 1997, during the survey of part of the quarry he located and uncovered a Saxon copper alloy hanging bowl and a single millefiori decorated mount. Further ferrous signals were noted in association with these pieces and exploratory excavation was carried out on what proved to be the Anglian grave.

The burial was announced widely within the media. This started with a press conference chaired by Professor Rosemary Cramp and Ian Meadows which resulted in a slew of publicity from 23rd April 1997 with television including Blue Peter recording the event as well as articles in national (Fig 1.4) and local newspapers (Fig 1.5). A half page cartoon by Chris Riddell was published in the Observer on 27th April 1997 which depicted the Prime Minister John Major placed in a grave with his 'grave goods' including a traffic cone and Margaret Thatcher's handbag which was used as his pillow. The importance of the Pioneer burial may be seen in that it has its own extensive Wikipedia page which can be found at: https://en.wikipedia.org/wiki/Pioneer_Helmet (accessed 25 May 2018).

The Pioneer burial artefacts were analysed and reported on by specialists. The items were conserved with the helmet fragments reassembled and placed in a fixed display (Fig 1.6).

The Pioneer burial artefacts were on temporary display in several museums including Northampton Borough's Central Museum and the New Walk Museum, Leicester before being loaned by Messrs Gammage and Minney to the British Museum (registration number AL. 226). These artefacts have subsequently been held on long term loan at the Royal Armouries Museum, Leeds. Replicas of the helmet have been made including by Tim Noyes of Heron Armoury (heronarmoury.co.uk). An initial replica was also made by Chris Smith of the Royal Armouries.

Interim reports were published in Current Archaeology (Meadows 1997) and Northamptonshire Archaeology journal (Meadows 1997). The client report was produced for the archaeological work to satisfy the planning requirements (Meadows 2004). This present publication has used the specialists' reports from the 2004 client report and these have not been updated. Any recent relevant discoveries since then will therefore not have been taken into account. In contrast this publication has progressed the 2004 client report in terms of textual information and illustrations in all the other areas from the background, excavation and especially the discussion.

Archaeological background

Prehistoric ceremonial and burial complexes have been found c1km to the south of the Pioneer burial. Here a Neolithic mortuary house, twelve Bronze Age round barrows and a possible long enclosure ceremonial monument as well as some pits containing four Bronze Age urns were excavated at Grendon Pit between 1974 and 1980 (Gibson and McCormick 1985; Jackson 1995).

Iron Age and Roman settlement sites have been recorded across the parish (RCHM 1979, 179-180). A Roman villa had been recorded c1.5km to the east of the location of the

FIGURE 1.4. DAILY MAIL ARTICLE DATED 23 APRIL 1997

FIGURE 1.5. ARTICLE IN NORTHAMPTON CHRONICLE AND ECHO DATED 23 APRIL 1997

Pioneer burial with a bathhouse and other features found during work for the Wollaston bypass (Chapman and Jackson 1992). This project also found an early Saxon site including a Sunken Featured Building (SFB) dating to the late 6th to early 7th century (*ibid*).

In the parish there was a single probable middle Saxon site immediately to the south-west of the then limits of Wollaston village and this was 2km to the east of the Pioneer burial (*ibid*, 180). Within the village occupation evidence dating from the 5th to the 14th centuries has been found at Dando Close (Semmelmann and Ashworth 2004). Four other sites in the village which produced middle Saxon pottery were at the churchyard, Beacon Hill, Priory Road estate, and the paddock behind Cromwell House in London Road (Hall 1977, 17).

Wollaston was recorded as Wilavestone in the Domesday Book which derives from Wulflāf's farm, v. tun (Gover *et al* 1975, 197). Wulflaf was a personal Old English name possibly representing the settlement's founder (Hall 1977, 21). Wollaston had two manors in 1066, Bury Manor which had five hides and was held by four thegns under Edward the Confessor and Hall Manor, about a quarter of the parish, which had been held by Stric in the same period (*ibid*, 47-49).

The Pioneer burial was found at Wollaston's southern parish boundary with Strixton parish, within *c*50m of a medieval feature called *Longhedge* (Hall 1977, fig 1). Longhedge had probably been planted when Strixton was taken out of Wollaston parish in the 12th century (*ibid*, 23). This boundary had still been maintained in the fields at the time of the excavation of the Pioneer burial.

It was also directly to the east of the land area called *Ryholme* which had anciently been partly ploughed and partly meadow, and surrounded by brooks. The burial

Figure 1.6. Helmet restored with Ian Meadows directly behind talking to colleagues (Greg Phillips, Graham Cadman, Vikki Pearson, Martin Ellison, Ian Meadows, Rob Atkins, Glenn Foard, Brenda Perryman, Jenny Ballinger and Ann Bond)

was to the east of one of these brooks called Swallow Brooke.

In the medieval period Wollaston had a three-field system which was recorded in 1370 (Hall 1977, 138), with the Pioneer helmet located in the Nether Field, and was in a furlong recorded as part of Forty Acres in 1774 (*ibid*, fig 4 and table 32), but prior to this was seemingly unnamed in records dating from after *c*1430 to 1774.

Topography and geology

The Pioneer site lay on an area of just above the broad flat river floodplain at about 46m OD, less than 1km to the south-east of the present River Nene, about 100m above the edge of medieval alluvial cover (Fig 1.1; NGR SP 8855 6275). The geology within the site was a light brown sandy silt with small quantities of gravel.

Chapter 2

Excavation

Burial location

The Pioneer burial was located *c*100m south of the nearest open excavation part of the Wollaston Quarry and on the other side of a hedge row to this archaeological work (Fig 1). This part of the quarry had been stripped of topsoil in preparation for being used for subsoil storage, rather than quarrying, and had therefore not been earmarked for any archaeological excavation. The burial itself was at the extreme edge of the stripped area and was found in March 1997 by Steve Critchley whilst metal detecting. He recorded strong signals over more than a 2m area and he exposed the top of the copper alloy hanging bowl. The author and Steve Critchley recognised the importance of the find and the area was then excavated as part of the watching brief contingency stipulated in the Brief (Kidd 1995, section 2.5; See Chapter 1).

The excavation methodology

The grave was carefully cleaned to expose its full extent. A temporary baulk, 0.2m wide, was kept across the grave at right angles to the long axis of the grave (Figs 2.1 and 2.2). It was not located across the centre of the grave, but positioned where the metal detector indicated there were no metal objects, directly to the south of an area which the metal detector had suggested contained a large iron object (found on excavation to be the sword). This temporary baulk was maintained across the burial and this was later removed at the end of the excavation.

Three trenches each 0.8m wide were excavated onto the natural subsoil extending at right angles from the burial on its eastern, southern and northern side (Fig 2.1). These were excavated in order to see whether there had been a ditch around the burial or if any other features were present. The size of the grave, and the status of the individual buried there, as reflected by the grave goods, might suggest that a barrow may originally have been present. The width of the grave was larger than an ordinary single Saxon grave, the single burials from Wakerley about 30km to the north, for example, were on average 0.75m wide (Adams *et al* 1989). However the detailed hand excavation in the vicinity of the grave pit and the machining of the three trial trenches did not produce any evidence of a barrow ditch, though this could have been erased by subsequent cultivation from the late Saxon or medieval periods (See Chapter 5, Discussion).

The ground at the time of excavation was dry and hard but the grave was excavated using wooden tools and soft brushes to minimise the risk of damage to the artefacts. All objects were photographed *in situ* prior to lifting.

The shallowness of the overburden covering the grave had resulted in the degradation of several of the artefacts by cultivation; the damage was most apparent to the helmet where plough entry and exit points could be identified. The process of cultivation would also have removed any artefacts that might have been higher within the grave.

The grave

The grave was a large shallow oval feature, aligned roughly north-west to south-east. It was 2.8m long and 1.3m wide, surviving to a maximum depth of 0.15m cut into the natural gravely clay (Figs 2.1 and 2.2). The grave was larger than a typical burial (but well within bed burial dimensions such as Swallowcliffe Down (Speake 1989)).

The sides of the grave dipped steeply to the slightly irregular base. Within the grave was a single adult aged to the early to mid 20s (See Wakely, Chapter 4). He had been laid roughly aligned south-west to north-east with his head on the south-western side. He was in a supine position but presumably owing, at least in part, to ground acidity and/or locally acid from any other objects such as bedding, he was represented by only limited skeletal fragments. The small size and isolated character of the surviving parts preclude detailed consideration of body posture.

The skull was the best surviving part of the body and was located *c*0.6m from the southern edge of the grave well away from its side. The skull lay somewhat upright within the grave, there were no signs of it having rolled backwards or of it having originally rested on its posterior surface (Fig 2.4).

It survived as a large fragment directly to the north of a copper alloy hanging bowl. This hanging bowl was deliberately placed between the head and the southern edge of the grave (Fig 2.5).

The relatively good preservation of the skull was presumably due to its close contact with the copper alloy hanging bowl as the effects of chemicals released by the bowl locally altering the soil chemistry in this part of the grave. Elements of both dental arcades survived and their respective grinding surfaces, although displaced laterally, were in the correct articulation. It would appear

The Pioneer burial

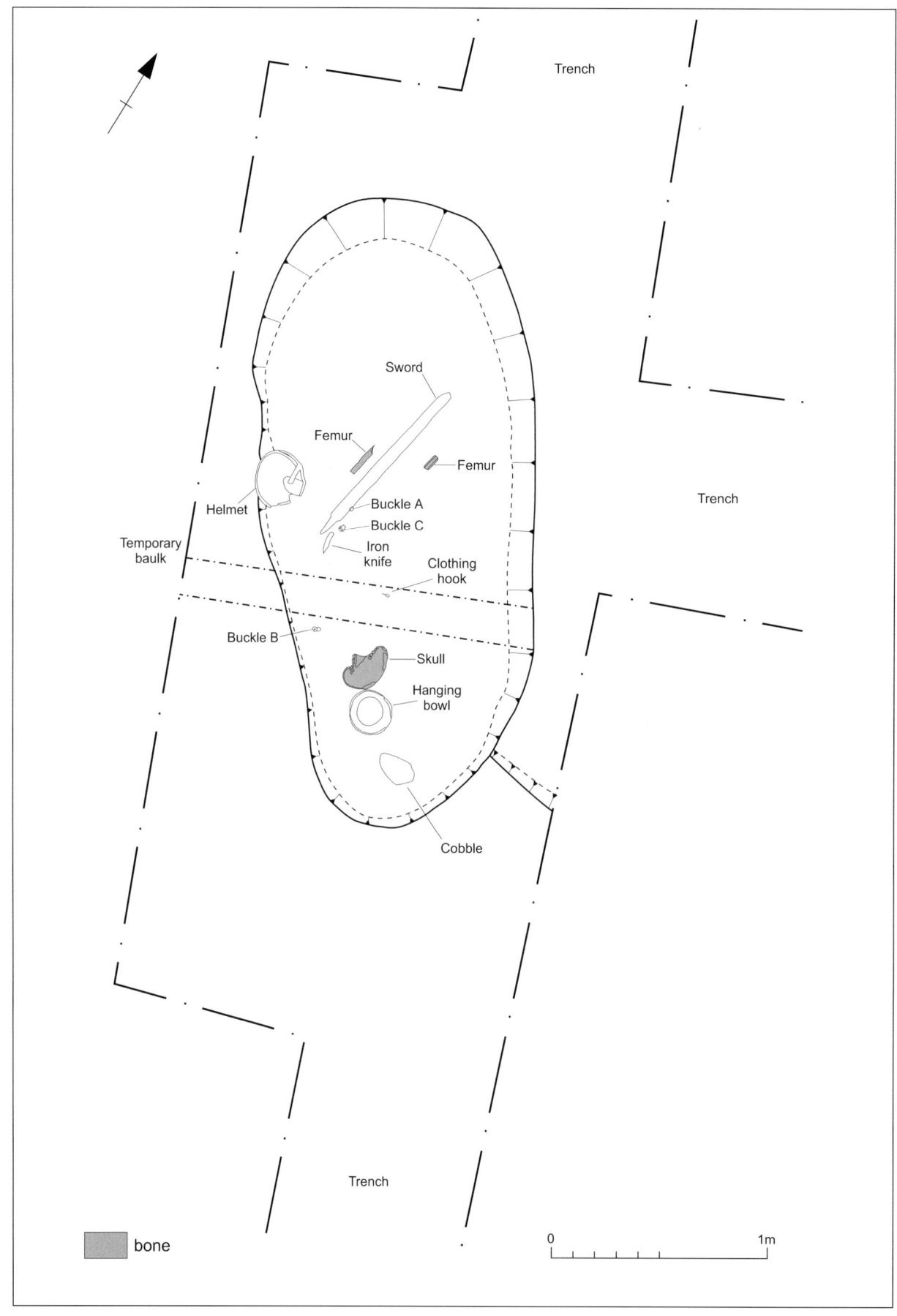

Figure 2.1. Plan of burial showing grave goods

Chapter 2 Excavation

FIGURE 2.2. VIEW OF THE BURIAL, LOOKING SOUTH

FIGURE 2.3. VERTICAL VIEW OF SWORD, FEMURS AND PART OF HELMET

that the head had not rolled or lolled but had gently twisted to the left, perhaps as a pillow or other headrest had degraded.

Fragments of the shaft of the right humerus were found when the 0.2m wide temporary baulk was removed at the end of the excavation. The humerus had been located near to a clothing hook but the remains were so fragile that it did not survive lifting and was therefore not recorded in the specialist report (See Wakely, Chapter 4). The left and right femora were all that survived of the rest of the body. The position of the two femur fragments perhaps reflect post depositional displacement, although they could indicate that the legs had originally been slightly flexed, with the legs bent and raised at the knee.

The grave goods

A number of objects were arranged in the grave pit around the body, comprising a sword, a copper alloy hanging bowl, a small iron knife and an iron helmet. Three iron buckles (A-C) probably come from various leather straps and belts that had decayed and a single small copper alloy hook probably attached to clothes was recovered from the upper chest region.

The bowl lay adjacent to the head and when found it lay slightly tipped away from but still touching the skull. The position was suggestive of something slipping off a pillow or similar support. Only a single mount

The Pioneer burial

Figure 2.4. Remains of the skull, looking south

Figure 2.5. Hanging bowl, skull and cobble, looking south-west

FIGURE 2.6. DETAIL OF SWORD GRIP AND KNIFE

was recovered and from its position on edge, with the enamelled surface facing west, it is probable that it had become detached from the side of the bowl perhaps as a result of ploughing which had also removed part of the bowl.

The sword lay diagonally across the lower body, the grip where the left hip would have been with the blade pointing to below the right knee. The blade had taken a slight curve following the base of the grave pit and its tip had been broken after deposition. The iron knife was located about 20mm from the grip and in a parallel axis, perhaps indicating that it had been inserted into the upper part of the sword scabbard (Fig 2.6).

The helmet lay about 200mm from the sword, adjacent to the left hip of the body. It lay on its left side and most of the right side had been lost through ploughing (Figs 2.7 and 2.8).

Buckle A lay near the left shoulder and its relationship with any sword attachment or baldric is uncertain. Its small size would appear to preclude its interpretation as part of a sword suspension arrangement and it should perhaps be considered as a clothes fastener. The position of the other two buckles (A and C) would suggest they had functioned as part of an adjustable distributor strap raising the scabbard up. Buckle B was probably attached to the scabbard whilst buckle C lay 80mm away adjacent to the shoulder of the sword blade.

A series of short iron rods was contained in the plough dragged material around the helmet. The copper alloy hook was recovered during post excavation from a soil sample taken from the shoulder/upper chest area so only the area of its origin can be identified. The 20 litre soil sample was taken to recover either carbonised plant material or small artefacts such as beads. It was washed through a series of graduated sieves down to a 0.5 mm mesh. No ancient organic material was recovered and the copper alloy hook was the only artefact present.

A large unworked bunter sandstone cobble, 0.2m by 0.12m in size, lay between the hanging bowl and the southern edge of the grave (Figs 2.1 and 2. 5). No other large cobbles were found within the grave's backfill, and it lay in a straight line with the skull and hanging bowl. Its location here may therefore have been by accident or could have been deliberately placed, but if the latter is the case the reason is uncertain.

It is entirely possible that other grave goods lay within the grave but have not survived in the archaeological record either due to later truncation and/or they were perishable.

Figure 2.7. Helmet from above

Figure 2.8. Helmet in ground from side

FIGURE 2.9. HELMET IN CLING FILM

FIGURE 2.10. PLASTER BEING APPLIED TO HELMET

If the likely position of the body is measured there is a notable amount of 'space' between the helmet, to the sword and to the northern edge of the grave where there were no archaeological remains recorded over a c0.9m by 0.7m area.

After cleaning and photography the larger objects were supported whilst they were raised, the sword on a plank and the helmet in a casing of plaster of Paris bandages with a cling film barrier layer and raised as a soil block (Figs 2.9 to 2.10). This plaster-covered soil block was first x-rayed at Newarke Houses Museum in Leicester, revealing the boar-crested helmet within. The objects were then examined at the museum's conservation laboratory (see Chapter 3).

After excavation of the burial further trenches were excavated by machine around the burial, but no evidence for a mound or other features were found only the natural subsoil (Fig 2.11).

FIGURE 2.11. MACHINE EXCAVATION TRENCHES AROUND THE BURIAL, LOOKING NORTH-WEST

Chapter 3

Artefacts

Overview

This chapter comprises reports on the artefacts, their conservation and organic material associated with them or other burial artefacts such as possible bedding which have only survived as textiles. The artefacts are reported separately in four sub-groups; respectively the helmet, hanging bowl, sword and the other artefacts are reported together. Any related conservation or other report have been recorded with their relevant sub-group.

The helmet
by Ian Meadows

The terminology used to describe the helmet will parallel that used in the report on the Coppergate helmet (Tweddle 1992). The Pioneer helmet comprises an iron cap and originally two cheek pieces. Slightly more than half of the helmet is present, predominantly the left side, but some parts are barely represented owing to plough damage (Figs 3.1-3.6). In the following description the use of left and right will be from the wearers perspective not the observers.

The iron cap is made from 11 separate elements riveted together. The frame of the cap is formed from a brow band with a nose to nape band and two lateral bands running from the brow band to the crown where they join the nose to nape band. The areas between these framing strips were originally infilled with four sub triangular plates of which two survive. A second nose to nape band and two further lateral bands, composed of a C-sectioned strip riveted to the outer surface, provides additional strength and rigidity. The nasal is formed from a continuation of the nose to nape band. Most of the surviving helmet is composed of iron replacement minerals, therefore it has not been possible to obtain measurements of plate thickness or trace chemistry.

The helmet is plain with no decoration apart from groups of three shallow incised lines that are scored into the surface along each edge of the lateral bands, the nose to nape band and the upper edge of the brow band. These lines are possibly decorative elements to conceal rivet heads or are perhaps to aid in the location of the rivets.

The helmet can be described by its component parts (Fig 3.7).

The brow band

The brow band would originally have extended almost around the head from eye to eye but only 330mm of the left side and back and a short, 25mm, section of the right front survived. The band is up to 82mm wide with both edges plain. Its surviving end is fixed to the back of the nose to nape strip with a single rivet (Fig 3.1). At the front where it passes behind the nose to nape band an overlap of about 7mm is present on each side of the nose to nape band leaving a gap of 60mm between the ends of the brow band. Both ends of the brow band at the front had been cut and shaped to form part of the eye cut out.

Very little of the bottom edge of the brow band survives, most of the edge having been removed by ploughing. However, the complete left eye cut out, part of the right eye cut out, the length above the left cheek guard and a short, 26mm long, isolated section of the back are present allowing confidence in the reconstruction of the original form (Fig 3.4). Where the cheek flap hinge is joined to the bottom edge of the brow band a slight cut in is present, presumably to allow articulation of the hinge.

The rear edge of the helmet's brow band is almost entirely lost through ploughing but the short section that did survive, when X-rayed, appeared to have part of at least 2 possible perforations on its damaged edge. The purpose of perforations in this position could only be to fix a neck guard of some type. The Coppergate helmet had a mail aventail/curtain, the Sutton Hoo had a more rigid aventail but no trace survived of any such material in this grave. The series of short rods with holes at their ends were initially thought to have been part of a neck guard however it is more likely that they are stiffeners from a belt or belts. In one of the possible scenarios for these rods it was considered that any neck guard was entirely organic, perhaps formed of leather with these rods fixed to the surface as strengtheners but no contemporary parallels exist for such an arrangement. The purpose, and on such a small length the existence, of the perforations is therefore uncertain.

Nose to nape band

The nose to nape band is nearly complete. At the back it is overlapped by the brow band by 10mm where it is fixed with two rivets (Fig 3.3). It and runs over the

The Pioneer burial

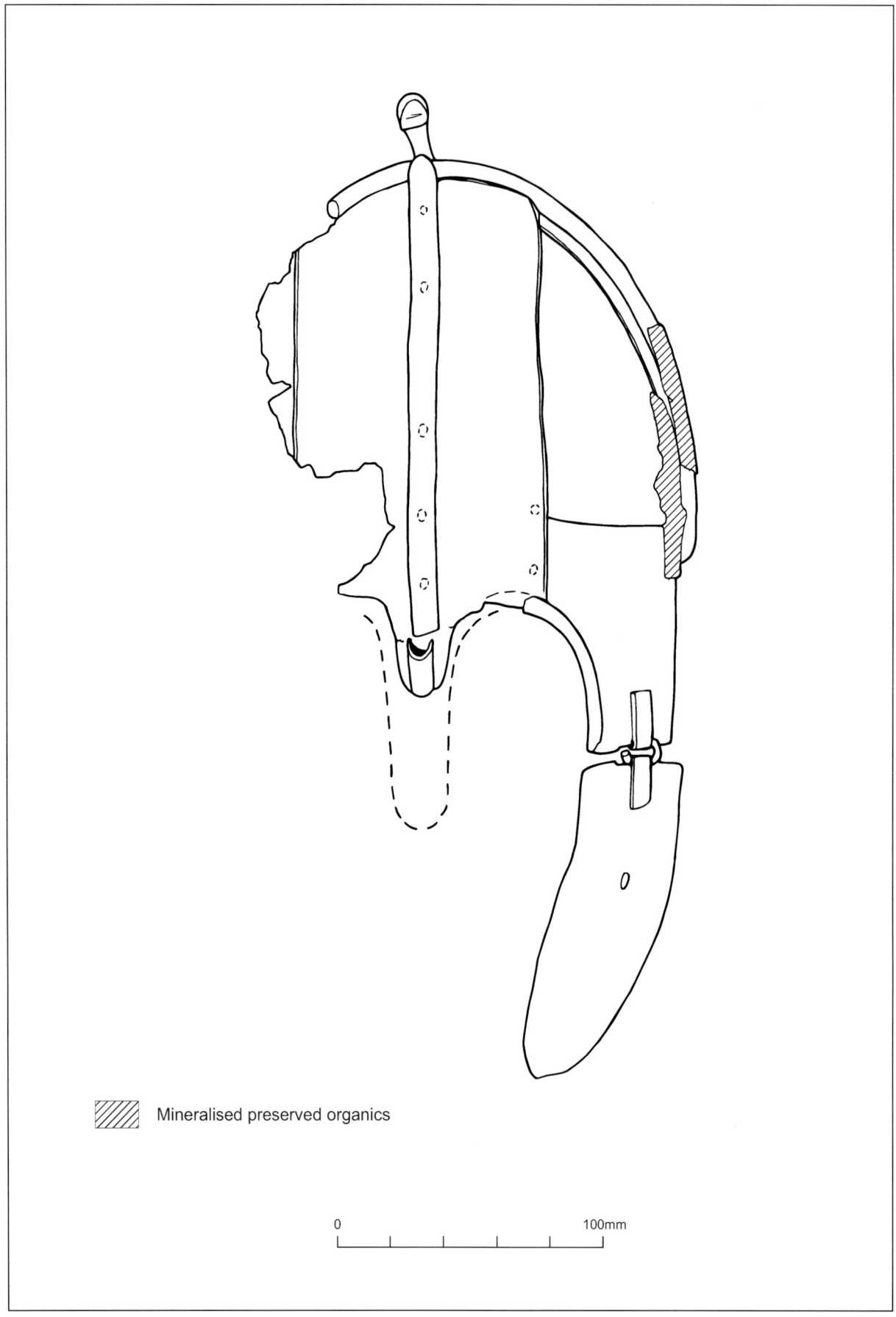

Figure 3.1. The helmet, front

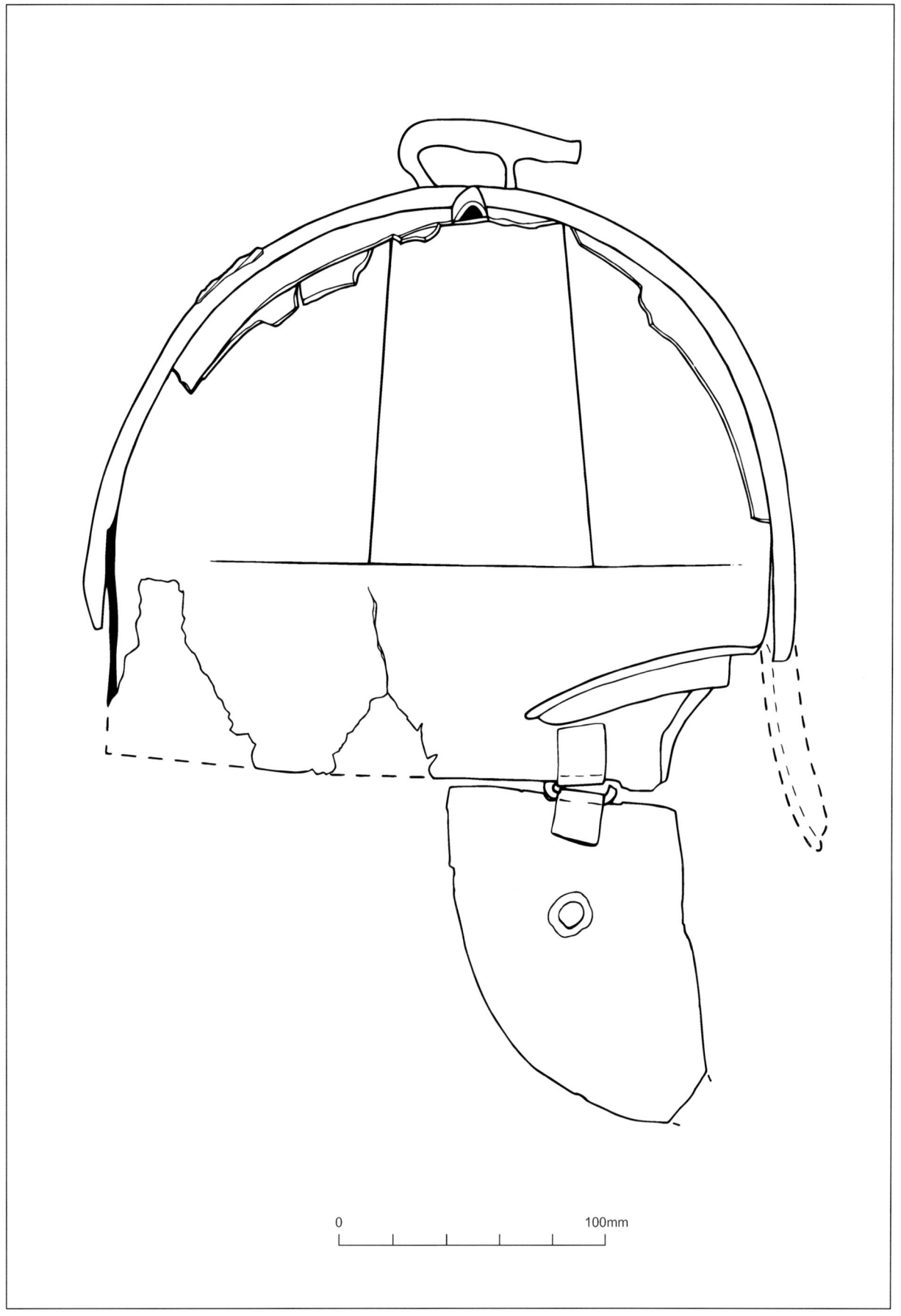

Figure 3.2. The helmet, right side, largely showing interior of left side

The Pioneer burial

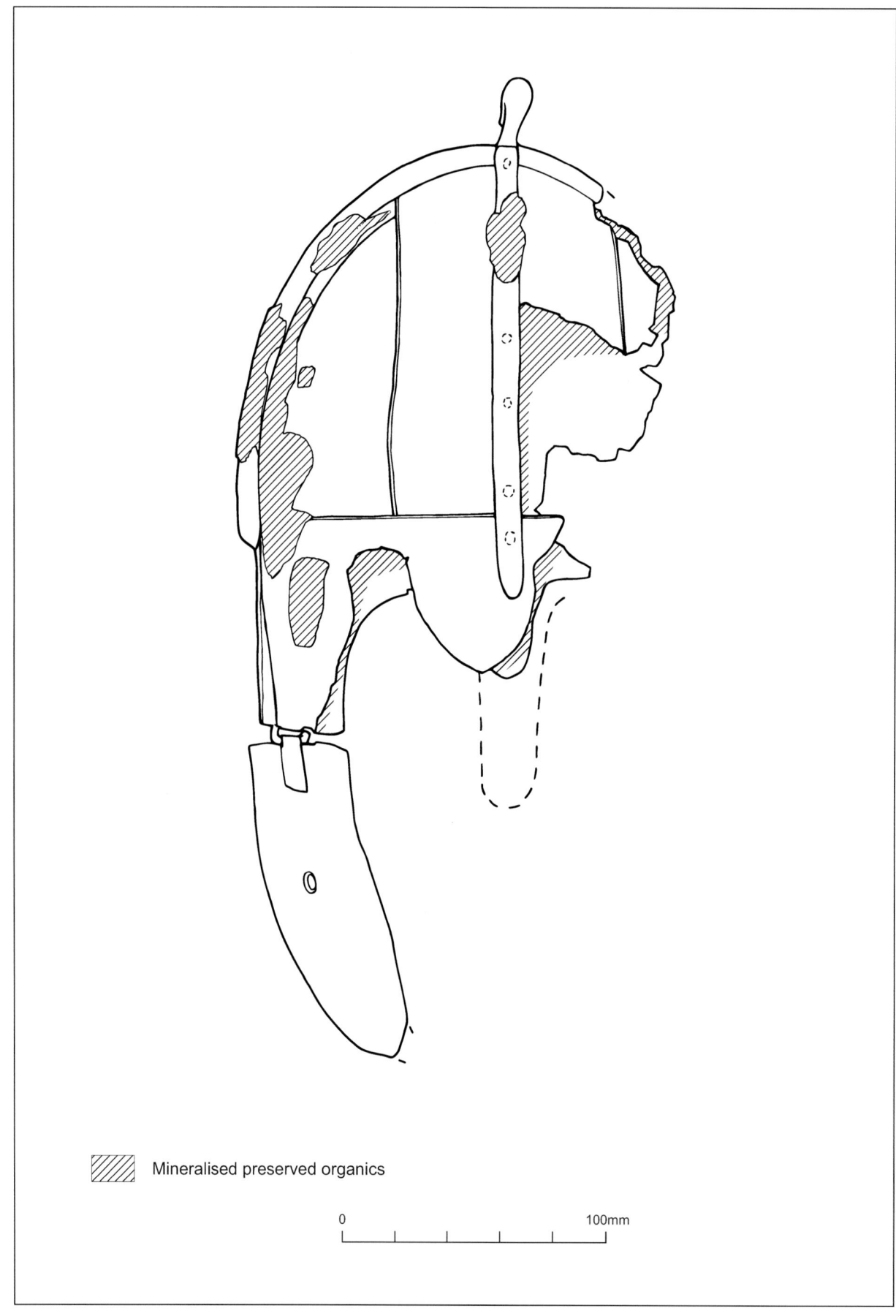

Figure 3.3. The helmet, rear

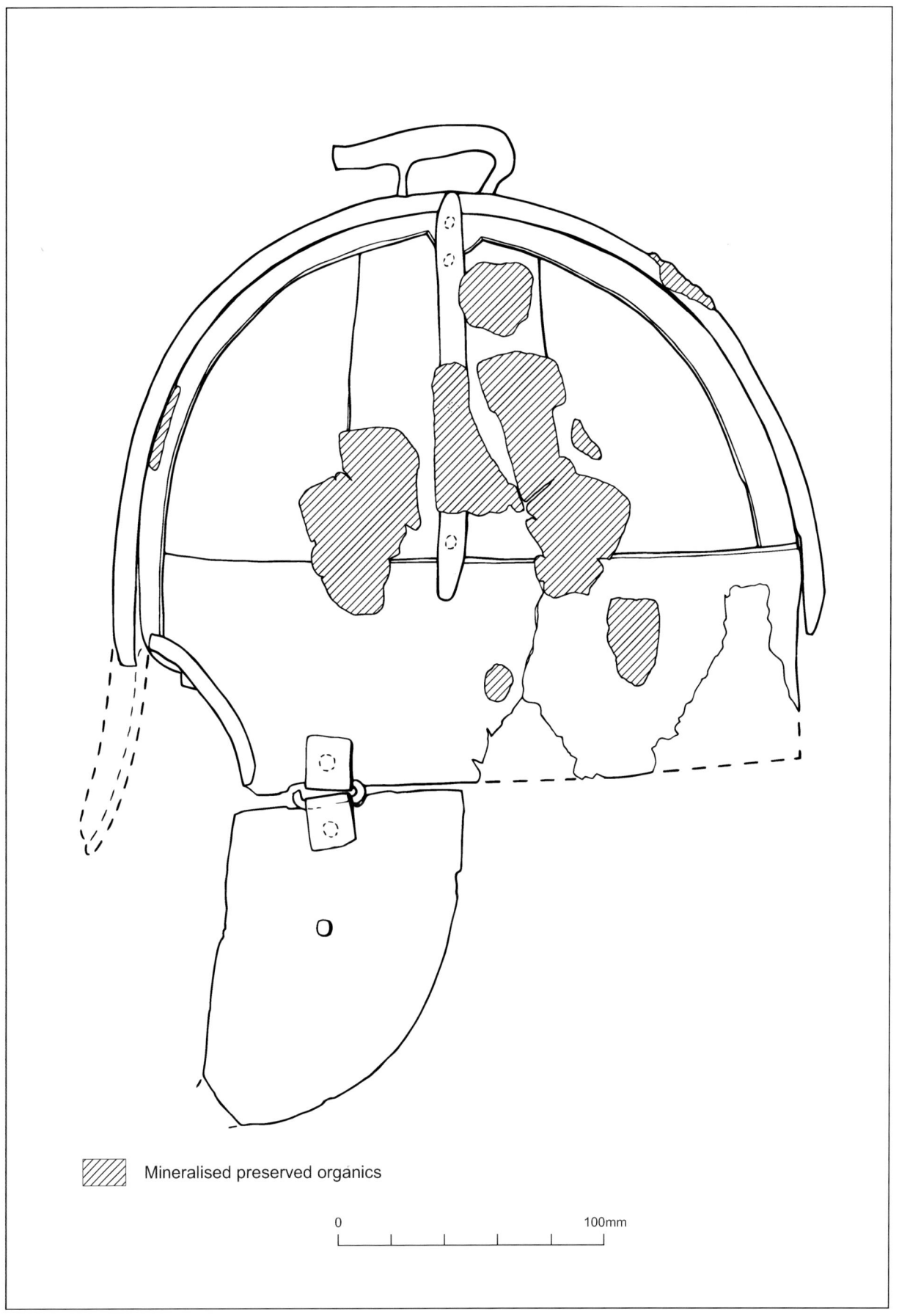

FIGURE 3.4. THE HELMET, LEFT SIDE

Figure 3.5. The conserved helmet

CHAPTER 3 ARTEFACTS

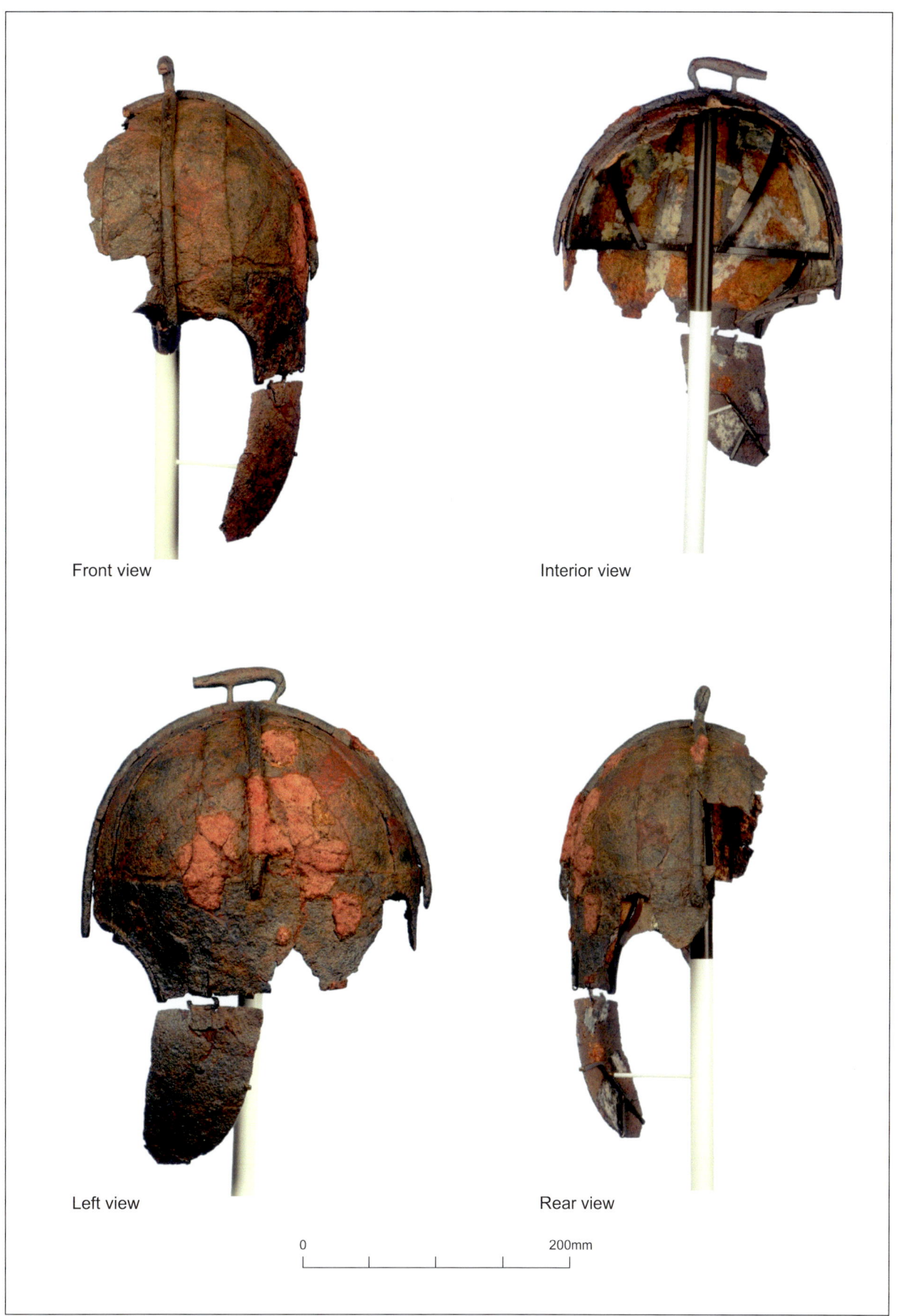

Front view

Interior view

Left view

Rear view

0   200mm

FIGURE 3.6. VIEWS OF THE HELMET FOLLOWING CONSERVATION

The Pioneer burial

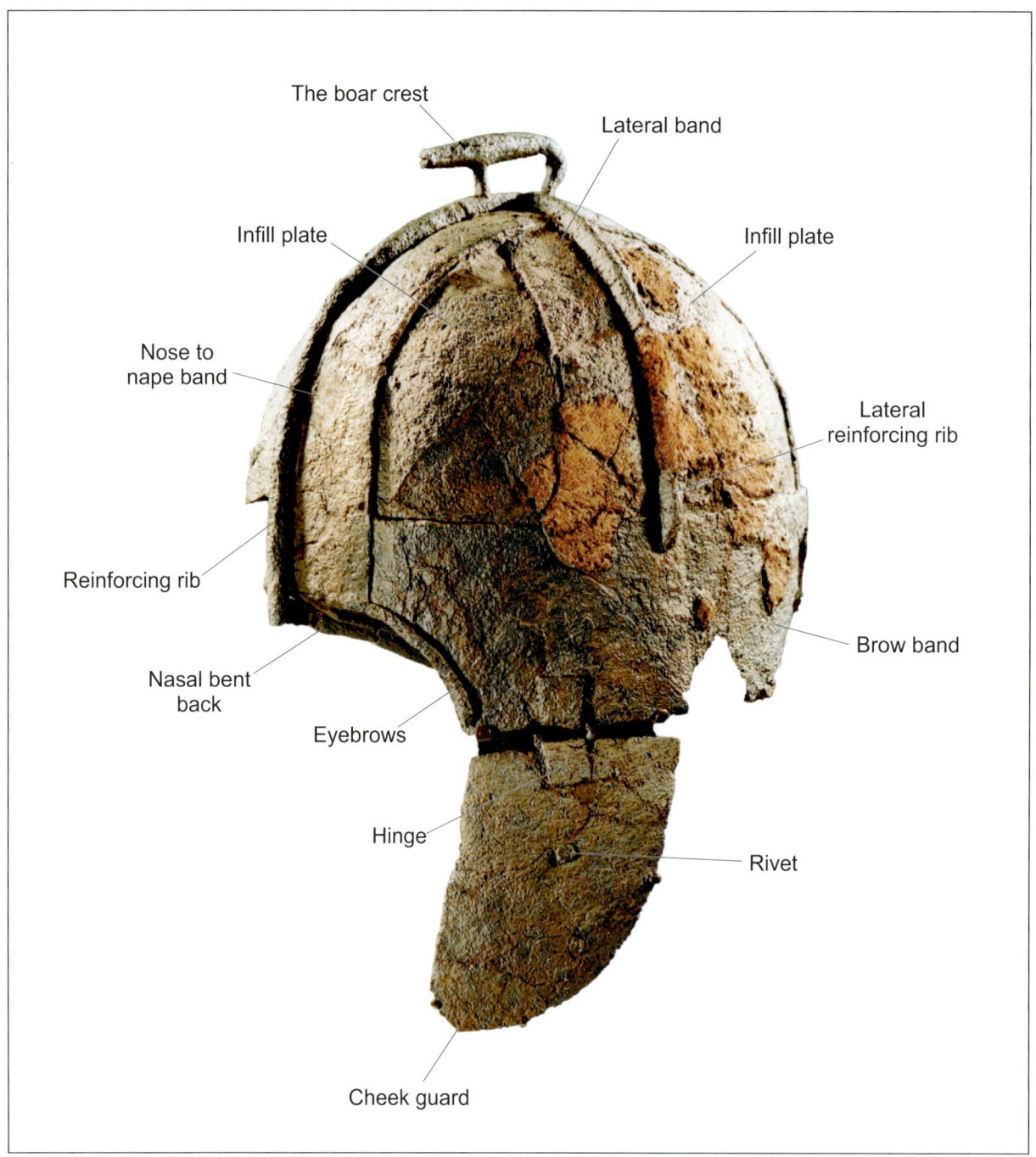

Figure 3.7. The helmet and its component parts

crown to the front where it overlaps the ends of the brow band. It has been cut and shaped for the eye cut outs and continues between them as the nose guard. The band is 415mm long and between 107 and 95mm wide. The edges of this strip are not straight reflecting the way they have been cut from a larger sheet. At the point where the left lateral band underlay the nose to nape band, a triangular extension to the nose to nape bands occurs (Fig 3.4). This triangle is 20mm wide where it extends out from the line of the band and it is 16mm high. The purpose of this extension is unclear however it would have added to the strength and rigidity of the construction.

Lateral bands

None of the right lateral band is present. The left lateral band is complete, c160mm long and flares from 69mm at the crown to 86mm wide at the brow band. It underlies the nose to nape band by c5mm and the brow band by 6mm (Fig 3.4). It was presumably fixed at each end by rivets.

External reinforcing ribs

Riveted to the nose to nape band and to the lateral bands are C-section applied ribs. The purpose of these ribs is almost certainly to provide further strength and rigidity to the construction. The nose to nape rib comprises a single piece that overlaps the edge of the brow band at the back by 30mm (Fig 3.3), it continues over the top and down the front on to, and forming part of, the nasal (Fig 3.1). On the right side the reinforcing rib survives only as a 36mm stub that abuts and slightly overlies the nose to nape strip (Fig 3.2). The left side is complete. It again abuts and overlies the nose to nape band and extends 12mm over the upper edge of the brow band (Fig 3.4).

The reinforcing ribs are presumably to increase rigidity; Chris Smith at the Royal Armouries in Leeds was able to confirm this during the production of a replica. The curve of these ribs, both with the curve of the cap and across its line give enormous rigidity to the whole construction. The ribs are riveted to the lateral bands and the nose to nape band.

The infill plates

The framework of the helmet left triangular spaces that were filled with pieces of sheet metal cut to size and shape. All four plates had been added to the inside and riveted to the frame formed by the brow and lateral bands. Both of the right infill plates are very fragmentary, only surviving at their junction with the nose to nape band (Fig 3.2).

The left plates measured much the same, the front example is140mm high and 95mm at the base and the rear example 137mm high and 95mm wide at its base. Both plates have near straight lower short edges but the long sides are curved to the apex. The plates are riveted through and one extends through three layers of metal. The frame overlaps the surviving plates by between 6-7mm (Figs 3.1-3.4).

The cheek guards

Isolated fragments that could not be reconstructed possibly represent the right cheek guard.

The left cheek guard was recovered in several joining pieces. It comprises a sub-triangular piece which curves in both the vertical and lateral plains giving the whole a curved and slightly convex form. It is 110mm long and up to 86mm at the top wide edge, the rear corner of this edge is bent outwards, which may reflect damage through use or might be a deliberate constructional detail allowing better articulation of the guard with the helmet.

The guard is suspended by a simple hinge from the lower edge of the brow band of the cap (Figs 3.4 and 3.8). The hinge is slightly to the front of centre on the cheek guard and comprises two strips of metal each 16mm wide folded over both the guard for about 17mm and the lower edge of the brow band. The strips of metal forming the

The cheek guard hinges

The boar crest

FIGURE 3.8. HELMET DETAILS

hinge are fixed by means of single rivets to either the guard or the brow band of the helmet. The two strips clamp a 25mm long but narrow loop made from 3mm thick iron wire; presumably this allows articulation of the guard and helmet. In order to accommodate the loop and provide closer fit, both sides are rebated into the edge of the cheek guard and the brow band.

A single large rivet is also present near the centre of the guard. The purpose of this rivet is presumably to secure fastening straps that would have tied under the chin, thereby securing the helmet. On the interior of the guard, parts of several fly pupae are present in the corrosion products.

The Pioneer burial

The eyebrows and nasal

The two eye openings each span two pieces of metal, the brow band and the nose to nape band. The right opening is only present at the point of its junction with the nasal but the left eye has the appearance of a high arch extending 52mm above the line of the base of the brow band and 51mm wide. Along the edge of the eye opening where it is part of the brow band a 5mm wide strip of metal has been riveted on. This strip has no apparent function other than decoration and balance, a rolled edge is present around the nasal, this strip continues its line. It overlaps the rolled edge of the nasal and extended to the edge adjacent to the cheek guard.

A 100mm length of the nasal had been bent back in antiquity (see below) however its original form is clear. The nasal, was part of the nape to nose band that is shaped to form the eye openings, it has a maximum length of 80mm and a width of about 21mm wide, terminating in a rounded end. Extending over the nasal is a continuation of the nape to nose reinforcing rib. The edge of the nasal is rounded over, possibly to thicken it or reduce the sharpness of the edge. This roll is about 5mm wide and extends from under the applied eyebrow strip all around the nasal. The bent portion is about 70mm long and bent inwards about 60° from the vertical. This act required sufficient force to fracture the reinforcing rib.

The Boar crest

A stylised boar, 68mm long and 24mm high, stands on the crown of the helmet (Fig 3.8). It is formed from a single rod of iron that has been forged to form a tapering curve at one end whilst the other had been split and one part bent down to form the forelimbs whilst the rest is further shaped to form the snout. The body of the boar is 12mm wide tapering to about 10m at the rear whilst the snout is 7mm wide. The boar figure is hardly formed beyond this stage although it was noted that the snout is worked to be more triangular and its end is slightly flattened 8mm across. No detail of eyes or mouth can be recognised. The boar is fixed to the reinforcing strip of the helmet and has clearly, during the helmets life, been bent slightly to the wearers' right.

The helmet in the grave

The helmet was found resting on its left side next to the left hip and prior to deposition it had been 'ritually killed' by the deliberate bending back of the nasal into the helmet, both fracturing the metal and rendering the helmet unwearable. The left cheek guard lay folded back into the helmet and when found it was overlain by the nasal, this however could to some extent be a reflection of post depositional compression.

The position of the helmet in the grave, resting on its side, resulted in the collection of water in the helmet interior. This process in turn facilitated the mineral replacement of organic material in the interior, some of which might represent padding and lining, unfortunately the quality of preservation was not as good as might have been hoped (see J Watson report below). The exterior surface of the helmet resting on soil just above the base of the grave had also preserved traces of organic materials, predominantly leather, probably from belts/straps and textiles probably from bedding (see P Walton-Rogers report below).

Conservation report on the helmet
by Anthony Read

The helmet came from the excavation in a soil block, supported by plaster bandages around 20mm thick. Initially it was unclear whether the artefact was a helmet or bucket. It was X-rayed extensively from every possible angle to build up a picture of what was contained within the soil block (Figs 3.9 and 3.10). X-rays revealed half an iron helmet with two ribs running front-to-back and ear-to-ear with a boar mounted in the centre of the crossover on the helmet crest. At this point, the thickness of the plaster and approx. 130mm of soil present made further interpretation of what was there very difficult. A separate

FIGURE 3.9. HELMET BEING X-RAYED

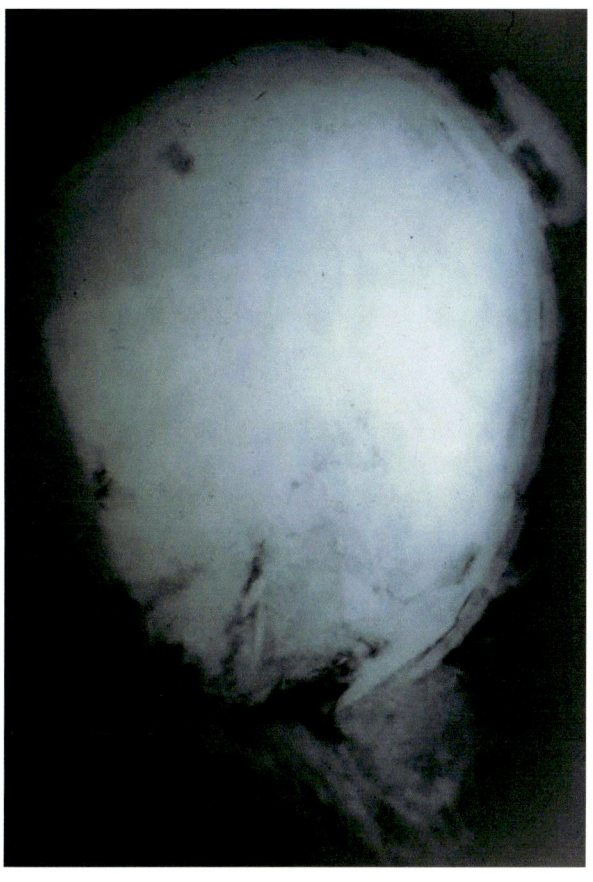

FIGURE 3.10. X-RAY OF HELMET

bag contained further fragments of the helmet, and another bag contained a sausage shaped piece of soil containing further pieces, found next to the helmet on the excavation and presumably caused by ploughing.

The helmet was badly compressed (the soil block was very shallow) and early indications were that it was very badly fragmented. The soil covering the outer face of the helmet was removed (bottom in the ground), cutting back the plaster of Paris casing as work proceeded, until the only plaster remaining was that supporting the helmet fragments. The outer face was then photographed (photography was carried out at regular intervals throughout the work; Fig 3.11). It was covered in cling film as a separating layer (all undercuts were filled with acid free tissue before the cling film was applied), and a new support made by casting two part expanding polyurethane foam onto it. The helmet was then turned over onto its new support, and the plaster of Paris jacket, which had been its support up to that point, was safely removed. Loose pieces were present at the front of the helmet, on the line of the ridge that runs under the boar, these were interpreted as the nosepiece.

Excavation of the interior of the helmet then began. Much of the right side of the helmet was lost due to later ploughing. In addition, a blow from the plough had entered at a lower level to the right of the boar,

FIGURE 3.11. HELMET BEING CLEANED

FIG 3.12. INTERIOR OF CHEEK GUARD AFTER CLEANING WITH PUPAE CASTS AROUND CENTRAL RIVET

dragging a trail of debris into the helmet exiting through the back of the left side of the helmet. There was debris behind the back of the helmet here that may represent what was present at the back of the head for protection. A cheek guard, much distorted and fragmented, was found inside the helmet, folded over on its hinge, which had broken (Fig 3.12).

The helmet was excavated as far as possible without removing the pieces inside it. These were then recorded by photography and the block was planned. The fragments of iron inside the helmet were then removed, pieces from different areas being kept together. Nick Gore and George Jeavons, representatives of Pioneer Aggregates, the clients of the project, visited to view the helmet at this point (Fig 3.13).

The 18 or so pieces into which the cheekpiece was broken were individually removed and reassembled using "HMG" a cellulose nitrate based adhesive, reversible in acetone. Although distorted in the ground the distortion appears to have taken place since the corrosion of the cheekpiece - when assembled the fragments of cheekpiece naturally took on what is presumed to represent their original shape. The breaks, though not fresh were not covered with very heavy encrustations with the exception of the area around the hinge. This area was extremely corroded both in terms of the state of the plate itself, and the joins of the fragments. This area only survived in a fragmentary state, with large areas of the plate lost.

Some of the other pieces appear to be fragments of the second cheekpiece which could have been hanging inside the helmet at the time of deposition and subsequently hit by ploughing. However the deposits present in the helmet are extremely fragmented, the edges of the pieces badly corroded and there is little chance of an accurate reconstruction. The identification of the possible right cheekpiece fragments was entirely on the basis of the shape of their edges.

The nosepiece survives, but is broken into a number of fragments, presumably again as a result of plough damage. It is bent back at right angles to the angle at which it would be expected to be found. The fragments have corroded into this shape - an indication that the bending took place prior to, or at the time of deposition (other distortion takes the form of movement in the gaps between the pieces rather than a change of shape in the fragments themselves). The joints in the nosepiece again survive sufficiently for it to be possible to piece the nosepiece together. The pieces were adhered with HMG. The rest of the soil within the helmet was removed. The helmet and fragments were then transferred to a low humidity store (at 15% RH) where it was dried out, and where it was stored when it was not being worked on.

The helmet, once dried out, was X-rayed again from a number of different angles, with and without intensifying screens and at a number of different exposures, to gain as much information as possible about its construction. It is very similar construction to the helmet found at Coppergate, York in the 1980s (Tweddle 1992). It consists of a brow band to which bands running over the head from nose-to-nape and from ear-to-ear have been attached. The gaps between these bands have been filled by triangular plates, and semi-circular ridges have been added on the midpoints of the nose to nape and ear to ear bands. The boar stands on the crossover of these semi-circular ridges (Figs 3.14 and 3.15).

The X-rays showed the helmet to be very badly damaged (it is broken into 100-200 fragments) and incomplete (75% of the right side is missing, as is the area at the back of the neck on the left side). The helmet has also opened up along the breaks and so, the pieces have distorted badly in the ground.

Figure 3.13. Nick Gore and George Jeavons inspect the helmet in Leicester

Figure 3.14. Unconserved boar crest

Figure 3.15. Detail of boar crest after cleaning

Areas of the main piece of the helmet, in the section that was uppermost in the ground, were very fragile and badly fragmented. The many cracks present in these parts, were injected with HMG, diluted 50% with acetone, in order to consolidate them and to prevent collapse from occurring.

The inner surface of the helmet was then carefully cleaned under the microscope using hand tools. Extensive organic remains were found, present in the corrosion products of the helmet's interior. These could perhaps represent the remains of the helmet's lining. The surface was cleaned to reveal them. Pieces of helmet that became detached during the process (by removal of the soil matrix which was all that held them together) were adhered in place with HMG.

The inside of the helmet in this form was then photographed and drawn. A number of samples were taken of the organic remains, the positions of which were recorded on the artist's drawing, for later analysis by scanning electron microscopy.

The pieces of the nosepiece were removed, taken apart with acetone, and restuck, again with HMG. The nosepiece, being of manageable size, was kept separate from the helmet at that stage and was treated as a single piece. No organic remains were present on it, so it was cleaned using 53 micro Aluminium Oxide powder in an air abrasive. Pale shadows on the X-ray did not represent a white metal coating instead they turned out to be a rolled area around the outer edge of the nosepiece, the extra thickness being to give this vulnerable area extra strength.

The surviving cheekpiece was also restuck using HMG and was cleaned in a similar way to the nosepiece. Organic remains (possibly leather) were found on the inside of the cheekpiece around the central stud and were left untouched, as were the insect pupae cases, also found on the inside surface of the cheekpiece.

The interior of the helmet was then cleaned to show its structural details. This was carried out with air abrasive, using 53 micro aluminium oxide powder as abrasive agent. Cleaning was only carried out in areas of the helmets which were likely to reveal structural detail

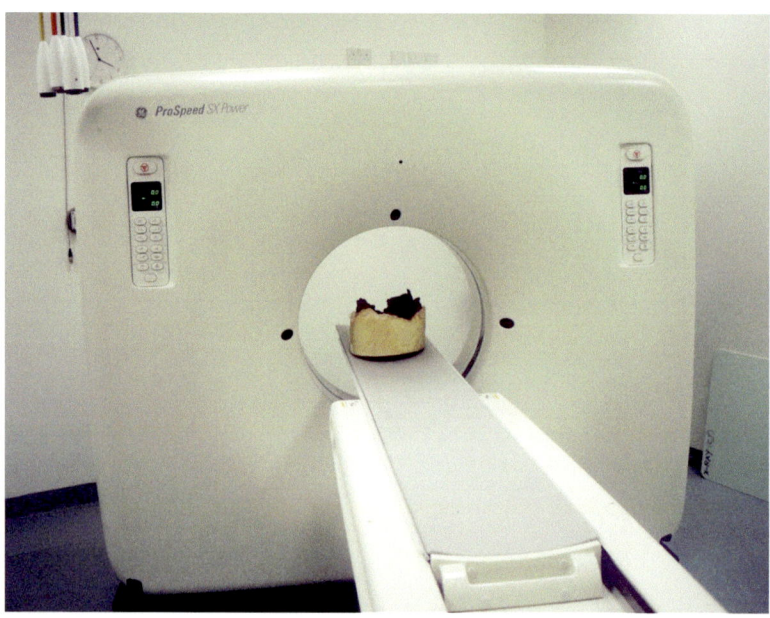

FIGURE 3.16. HELMET IN CT SCANNER

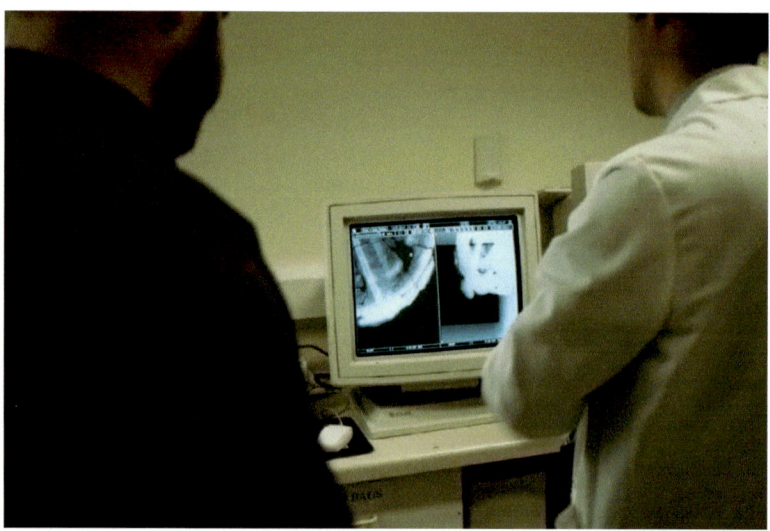

FIGURE 3.17. RESULTS EXAMINED ON COMPUTER

(e.g. the backs of the central nose-to-nape and ear-to-ear ridges, looking for rivets, the areas where overlapped and joined, to give the shapes and thicknesses of these plates, and other areas e.g. under the boar, where it was felt information might be gained. This strategy was carried out, in order to reveal as much of the detailed construction of the helmet as was possible, without totally destroying other organic remains of the lining. Around 50% of the helmet's interior was left unabraded.

CT scans were taken of the helmet before the work started, showed that areas of the helmet were very heavily corroded, the surface being extremely fragile and porous (Figs 3.16 and 3.17). These areas were not cleaned quite as vigorously as the others. Holes made in the porous surface were filled with pigmented HMG to prevent them from increasing in size as work progressed.

A mount was made for the inner face of the helmet with expanding 2 part polyurethane foam, using clingfilm as an intervention layer, and the helmet was turned over to reveal the outer surface. The outer face was covered in extensive areas of mineralised organic - principally:-

- Textile, over the central area.
- Leather on the back of the boar and the rear portion of the central ridge.
- Feathers (just the central spines) above the eyebrow.

The initial provisional identification of the feathers was made but unfortunately the samples taken for detailed analysis proved to be root. Other types of organic i.e. the leather on the ridge and the textile was left in situ and was not cleaned off later.

The helmet was partially assembled from its constituent pieces at this point, to give around 7 large parts of manageable size. The methods of stabilisation into a piece were: - badly fragmented areas - injection of HMG, diluted 50% with acetone into the cracks. Areas with larger and more robust pieces - cleaning of corrosion present onto the joints with air abrasive and assembly with HMG adhesive.

The larger pieces were then cleaned in the same manner as the cheek and nosepieces with 53 micron aluminium oxide powder in an air abrasive unit. During the cleaning of all the exterior surfaces of the helmet, decoration was found in the form of groups of 3 parallel grooves, present about 3mm in from the edges of all the plates except the lower edge of browband and the triangular fill plates. These grooves were very faint, due to the extensively corroded nature of the helmet and can only been seen in small sections, on very careful examination of the remains.

The helmet was then reconstructed:

The larger sections were disassembled as required and reassembled in such a way that the different parts of the helmet fitted together and "locked". The more fragile and heavily fragmented areas were simply softened with HMG where they needed a little reshaping and it was felt that disassembly would result in damage to them. Fragile areas were backed with glass fibre matting, covered in HMG to given them added strength.

When the assembly of the different components of the helmet was completed, all the weak joints and fragile areas were reinforced with glass fibre matting and HMG in this way to give strength of the helmet and reduce the fragility of the most badly damaged areas. The gaps in the helmet were also spanned by means of glass fibre and HMG in order to give a backing to which gapfill could be applied. Gaps and large cracks in the helmet were gapfilled with a mixture of Primal WS24 acrylic emulsion (dissolves in acetone when set), aluminium oxide powder (53 micron) and pigment (lamp black and titanium dioxide). The background colour of this filler was a charcoal colour. Gapfilling was only carried out in order to improve the appearance and strength of those parts of the helmet that survived (so that the eye of the museum visitor would not be drawn to the cracks and voids). No attempt was made to reconstruct the missing areas of the helmet.

The filled panels were then blended in with the original material. It was decided that a close match in colour, only distinguishable from the original on close examination, was the most appropriate way of painting the infill panels. The panels were painted with a pattern of tiny brown spots in acrylic paints (which dissolve in acetone). These tiny spots are invisible from a distance, giving the appearance of archaeological iron, but close up are recognisable as spots, revealing the inpainted areas of fill (they were applied to a charcoal coloured background).

The last action in the conservation of the helmet was the reattachment of the boar, which was cleaned separately, since it was a separate and complete piece in the helmet's fragmented form. The boar was adhered with Devcon 5 minute epoxy resin, pigmented to the colour of iron. This is the only piece of the conservation of the helmet not easily reversible in acetone. Epoxy resin was used because the boar was heavy and the point of attachment small. It was one of the most important parts of the helmet and one of the most vulnerable and so, it was considered necessary to use an epoxy resin for this job because of the extra strength given epoxy resins to joints.

Organic material associated with the helmet
by Jacqui Watson

The iron helmet was found in a fragmentary condition, so it was block lifted for detailed excavation at Leicester Museum's conservation labs by Antony Read. During the course of investigative conservation he took a series of samples of mineral preserved organic material for further examination.

Ten samples were taken from the interior of the helmet. Samples 1, 3-5, and 9 may be leather, but at high magnification on the SEM (scanning electron microscope) no diagnostic features could be found to confirm this. Unfortunately samples 2, 6-8, and 10 had no obvious organic structure at low magnification, and just appeared to be lumps of corrosion. Samples taken from the back of the boar on the helmets crest also turned out to have no obvious structure, other than a compacted surface, so could possibly be leather. Another sample taken from above the eyebrow, and thought to be feathers, turned out to be just a fragment of modern root.

Hanging bowl
by Lloyd Laing

The bowl (Fig 3.18), when complete, measured approximately 175mm in diameter and stood about 80mm high. As found, it comprises the main body of the vessel together with three detached rim sections, of which one has a rivet and 'washer' made from a cut piece of metal and the others rivet holes. Additionally surviving is a basal print, averaging 26mm in diameter. The bowl has an omphaloid base, slightly thickened in the centre where the basal print was attached. It is badly damaged, all the escutcheons now being missing, and was probably old when it was buried. There are scars on the inside and underside of the base, where basal prints were attached, one of which survives. There are two scars on the side of the bowl, probably where escutcheons were attached. There is a group of four perforations in a roughly triangular arrangement at one point under the rim, and a further perforation about one-third of the circumference from them in a similar position. It would appear likely that the bowl had the usual arrangement of three escutcheons for suspension, originally soldered to the vessel, but that attachments may have been riveted on as replacements at a secondary stage.

The bowl has a slightly thickened, flattened rim, incurved to a high shoulder (Fowler 1968). This profile is similar to that on the Chessell Down, I.O.W. bowl (Brenan 1991, cat 16) and to that on the Garton Slack, Humberside vessel (Brenan *op cit* cat 29). It is also quite closely related to the rim on the Finningley, North Yorkshire example which has a slightly more inturned lip (*ibid*, fig 1.3). The Garton Slack bowl is a vessel with enameled escutcheons in a 'Romanizing' style, while the Finningley bowl has been seen as a Roman product by writers since Kendrick (Kendrick 1932; Laing 1993).

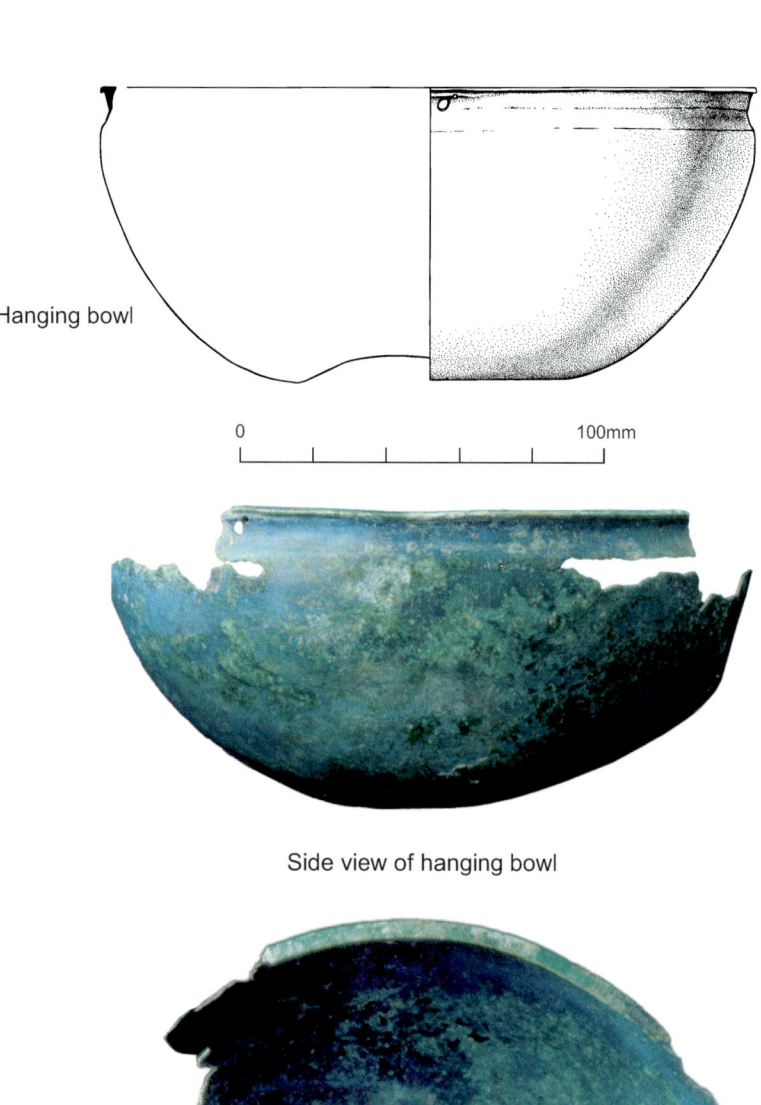

Hanging bowl

Side view of hanging bowl

Base view of hanging bowl

Escutcheon plate

FIGURE 3.18. HANGING BOWL

The surviving basal print, which averages 26mm in diameter, has champlevé red enamel, now partly missing, set in a field keyed to take it by scoring. Originally it would appear that there were about 24 squares of millefiori arranged in lines with patterns of blue and yellow squares in two designs, simple, made with larger rods, and more complex, with fine rods. The arrangement of the millefiori on the Wollaston bowl is otherwise unique in the hanging bowl series, though it is not unlike the arrangement found on some Roman disc brooches and discs (Bushe-Fox 1926). That this type of millefiori originated in Roman workshops and continued to be produced in the 5th and 6th centuries has been argued by the present author (Laing 1999). Carroll, while agreeing the origin was Roman, has suggested that it reappeared in the 7th century (Carroll 1995). The other examples of hanging bowls with millefiori inlays comprise those from Barlaston, Staffordshire, from 'Northumberland', from Barton, Cambridgeshire and a small later group with more complex millefiori from Sutton Hoo and Ipswich, Suffolk, Manton Common (Scunthorpe), Lincolnshire and on the lost bowl from the river Witham, Lincolnshire (Laing 1999).

It has been clearly demonstrated that all the depositions of hanging bowls in Saxon graves belong to the 'Final Phase' assemblages of the 7th and early 8th centuries (Geake 1999a). Arnold's 6th century deposition date for the Chessell Down bowl (Arnold 1982) has now been questioned by Geake (Geake 1999a), who has argued that it is more likely that the grave from which it came belongs to the early 7th century. It is apparent that although the presence of hanging bowls in Saxon graves can be seen to indicate a 7th or 8th century date for the assemblage in which they are found, the graves do not provide a date for the hanging bowls themselves, which could have been manufactured long before they became selected as appropriate grave goods for Saxon burials. How old the bowls may have been is a matter of guesswork, but the presence of old, damaged bowls in some of the early 7th-century graves (such as Sutton Hoo) suggests that they were made at least as early as the late 6th century, and that they were not produced for deposition in Saxon graves or indeed as status symbols for the 7th-century Saxon élite. Most recent commentators have suggested the production began in the 6th century – late 6th century according to Youngs (Youngs 1998), possibly early 6th century according to Dark (Dark 2000). Given the probable Roman origin of hanging bowls, and the growing evidence for continuing Roman technology in the 5th century, it seems hardly necessary to argue that there was a break in their production in the 5th century simply because we cannot assign any individual bowls to that period because they have not come from 5th-century archaeological contexts. That the technology necessary for the production of hanging bowls was still available in the 5th century is apparent from New Market Hall, Gloucester, where a fragment of an enameled bowl with geometric cloisons was found with a penannular brooch pin and various pieces of scrap associated with some sherds of a North African amphora dated to the 5th century (Hassall et al 1974).

Analysis of the hanging bowl
by Matthew Ponting

Scientific examination

The scientific examination of the bowl fragments consisted of microscopic examination of the metal structure by optical microscopy and examination of the perforations by scanning electron microscopy (SEM). Chemical analysis was conducted by energy dispersive analysis in conjunction with scanning electron microscopy (SEM-EDS) and inductively-coupled plasma atomic emission spectrometry (ICP-AES). The SEM used was a Jeol IC845 scanning microscope with an Oxford Instruments pentafet SiLi energy dispersive detector and Isis 200 processor system. The operating parameters were an accelerating voltage of 25 kV, counting for 200 seconds to give approximately 2000 counts on cobalt metal. The limits of detection are in the order of 0.1% depending on element. The ICP system used was a Perkin Elmer Plasma 400 sequential instrument calibrated with matrix matched multi-element standards. The limits of detection are in the order of 0.001% again depending on element.

Microscopic examination

The three detached rim sections all have evidence of piercings that were probably rivet holes for the attachment of the escutcheons from which the bowl was hung. The spacing of the piercings supports the suggestion that the bowl was old by the time it was buried and that at least two sets of escutcheons had been attached during the bowls working life. Rim section #2 fits with the left side of the remaining bowl, whilst rim section #3 fits with the right side. The third sections cannot be joined but probably belongs to the opposite side of the bowl. A microscopical study of the piercings and remaining rivets in the detached rim section was conducted in an attempt to understand the grouping and sequence of piercings.

Rim section #2 has a rivet and 'washer' made of an irregularly cut piece of sheet metal at one end and a hole and rivet at the other. Both rivets and the 'washer' are made of bronze rather than copper or brass. The hole is neatly drilled rather than punched and has been widened by use with the edges splayed by rubbing with a hard material. Another piece of rim (#3) has two piercings adjacent to each other at one end and which are neatly drilled round holes with very little sign of wear. Additionally there is a large hole at the opposite end that appears to have been heavily worn into an oblong shape by use. However, this hole is in the thin body metal of the bowl and could be the result of localised corrosion.

The twin holes on rim section #3 are located in such a way as to suggest that they formed part of a repair and this suggestion is supported by the relatively un-worn appearance of the holes.

Visual examination of the surface of the bowl revealed no evidence of planishing, although it seems likely from the metallography that the bowl was produced by raising. There is no clear evidence for turning on a lathe. The rim and the bowl are part of the same piece of metal indicating the high degree of technical skill that was required in the manufacture of these bowls. Metallographic study of a cut section from rim section #2 revealed a porous structure of small equiaxed grains with many of these showing annealing twins. Some strain lines and deformation are visible showing that working had continued after the final anneal. This is indicative of heavy cold-working and repeated cycles of annealing of the sort that is consistent with forming by raising.

Chemical analysis

Chemical analysis by SEM-EDS of rim section #2 and a fragment of the bowl body produced almost identical results confirming that the bowl was raised from a single piece of bronze. The alloy is a tin bronze containing approximately 10% of tin and 3.5% of lead. Minor contaminants detected were less than 0.5% of zinc and traces of iron and nickel.

The basal escutcheon has quite a different composition, containing approximately 8% of tin, 3% of lead and 1.5% of zinc. This piece was clearly made separately to the main body of the bowl, but of an alloy that was probably regarded as essentially the same. The small amount of zinc present, probably from contaminated scrap, would not have affected the alloy colour to any significant degree; neither would the small difference in tin content. The escutcheon was fixed to the bowl with a soft solder, traces of which remained to be semi-quantitatively analysed. This proved to be a tin-rich material, consisting of approximately 75% of tin and 25% of lead.

A small piece of the main bowl body was also removed for analysis by ICP-AES and was carefully prepared by the removal of the surface layers with a fine file. The results are in good agreement with the SEM-EDS analyses when differences in sample preparation are considered. The slightly higher tin content in the SEM-EDS analysis can be attributed to enriched surface material being unwittingly included in the analysis area and increased iron may result from slightly corroded areas being similarly included. Other discrepancies may well be due to the heterogeneity of the alloy. Trace elements not detected by SEM-EDS are relatively insignificant; arsenic is present at only 0.128%, antimony at 0.080% and silver at 0.075%. Other typical trace contaminants such as cobalt, gold and manganese are all below the detection limits of the technique as recorded in the table. Such an elemental profile would suggest fairly clean metal that was probably mostly recycled from carefully selected scrap. Repeated recycling tends to remove oxidizable trace contaminants, dependant on the chemical reactivity of the individual elements.

Discussion

There is a growing body of analyses of hanging bowls of varying quality. The analyses of eleven bowls were consulted during the course of this study, not including the well-known and detailed analyses of the three Sutton Hoo hanging bowls by the British Museum Department of Scientific Research (Oddy *et al* 1983). In all cases the alloy of the bowl body was bronze with only two analyses reporting more than 0.5% of zinc (1.5% and 2% respectively) and lead contents ranging from about 1% to 5%. The composition of the Wollaston bowl fits well with these other analyses and clearly conforms to what is starting to appear as if it is a fairly tight-knit and consistent range of compositions. The basal escutcheon is also consistent with a number of the basal escutcheons associated with other bowls; the enameled escutcheon of Sutton Hoo bowl No. 2 is reported to contain 9% tin, 1.7% zinc and 3.5% lead and the escutcheon from the Willoughton bowl (Brenan 1991, 152) is classified as a tin bronze by semi-quantitative X-ray fluorescence analysis. The presence of zinc in some of the bowls is probably due to the unavoidable inclusion of contaminated scrap metal in the re-cycling process, although the low levels of this suggest a fairly efficient selection process. Likewise, the amounts of lead have been kept at a level that would not interfere with the raising technique; larger amounts of lead would cause cracking and other flaws. Care would be needed in the selection of scrap metal that was low in lead as most late Roman castings could have contained up to 30%. Any argument for the use of primary, freshly smelted metals for these alloys is untenable because of the rarity of British copper sources that contain zinc and because the low levels of other trace contaminants in the alloy are consistent with metal that has been frequently re-cycled. There is one known British copper source that yields ores that do contain zinc, that in the Welsh Borders at Llanymynech and Llwyn Bryn-dinas in Montgomeryshire and Denbighshire respectively and which have been matched to Iron Age smelting remains (Northover 1991 and *pers comm*). However, low levels of zinc (< 2%) are encountered in hanging bowls and other insular bronzes of this period from a variety of disparate locations suggesting that the zinc is more likely to be contamination through re-cycling and not evidence for any particular ore source.

Unfortunately the Wollaston bowl has lost its rim escutcheons; these are decorative attachments that in some cases have proved to be made of brass (such as those on the bowls from Sutton Hoo, St. Pauls, Lincoln and Buiston, Ayrshire) or of high-tin bronze (one of the Sutton Hoo bowls), an alloy containing between 15 and 25% of tin. The use of such alloys for the decorative rim escutcheons is consistent with the view that such alloys were regarded as special and possibly exotic and were therefore used sparingly to decorate high-status objects. The use of these alloys is also significant because, as far as current knowledge is concerned, brass and high-tin bronze are rare alloys in the early Saxon period. Whilst reliable quantitative analyses of early Saxon copper-alloy metalwork are relatively few and far between, the data that are available suggest that there was a gradual decline in the use of brass during the late Roman period, with the lowest incidence of brass occurring in the immediate post-Roman/early Saxon period (AD 400-650). Interestingly enough, this same period apparently sees almost no use of copper and the highest incidence of gunmetal (mixed alloys containing several percent of both zinc and tin). All these factors point convincingly to a period of intense re-cycling with little or no fresh-metal production. This is particularly relevant to brass and reinforces the notion of a post-1st century decline in brass manufacture, partially off-set by selective re-cycling. This is indicated by the decline in zinc content; brass will loose approximately 10% of its zinc content on every re-melt (Caley 1964) and dilution by mixing with bronze and copper would further reduce the zinc content. It is also significant that there is an accompanying decline in the use of copper both because of its role as one of the raw materials for high-zinc cementation brass production and as an indicator of fresh metal supplies from mining. The overall picture to date therefore seems to be that there was no brass production during the early Saxon period; what brass there was came as a result of re-cycled earlier (Roman) and imported (Coptic?) metalwork. Thereafter, brass use appears to increase during the later Saxon periods, but still on a relatively small scale with bronze now being the usual copper-alloy at the expense of mixed alloys (gunmetal). Other data, however, suggests a slightly different picture where mixed alloys containing significant proportions of both zinc and tin (gunmetals) were the norm for early Saxon metalwork with the occasional brass object appearing (Mortimer et al 1986), but the picture is as yet far from clear, other than to show that brass was an uncommon alloy amongst the early Saxons. Nevertheless, there is a clear and striking contrast with continental Europe, where brass was consistently common (Oddy et al 1983). A beaded rim Frankish type bowl from Empingham was analysed alongside the Wollaston bowl for comparison. These bowls are generally dated to the late 4th and 5th centuries AD (Oddy et al 1983, 945), although the Empingham example comes from a burial containing a brooch dated to between 500 and 525, presumably reaching Rutland through trade (Cooper 2000, 27-30). The analysis (by SEM-EDS) of a cut section from the rim of the bowl revealed a composition of 13% zinc, 5% tin and less than 1% of lead. This is a particularly zinc-rich gunmetal that could be termed a low-zinc brass. Such compositions are typical of late Roman and Byzantine copper-alloys (Unglik 1991, Ponting 1999) and clearly represent a very different alloying tradition to that of the hanging bowls, one that is based on the unselective re-cycling of brass and bronze (Ibid 1999). In Scotland and other parts of the 'Celtic fringe' a picture seems to be emerging where both brasses and gunmetals are rare and bronze is the norm, together with some un-alloyed copper (Eremin et al 2002; Bayley 2000). This would seem to indicate that fresh metal was available in some regions, and is indeed borne out by evidence for tin production in Cornwall during this period (Penhallurick 1986).

Thus the apparent 'purity' of the alloys used for hanging bowls and their fittings appears rather at variance with the contemporary Saxon metalwork. However, this should be of no surprise, for when comparisons have been made between the metalwork of some of the different cultural groups at this period an interesting picture begins to emerge (Craddock 2001). The use of a reasonably tight range of 'clean' bronze compositions for the hanging bowls has strong similarities with the copper-alloys produced in the 'Celtic fringe' such as those reported by Bayley from 7th century Dunadd (Bayley 2000, 208) and the later 8th to 10th century metalwork from pagan Norse graves in Scotland (Eremin et al 2002). This certainly connects hanging bowls with indigenous British pre-Roman alloying traditions and marks them out compositionally from Saxon, Scandinavian and Merovingian metalwork that followed the late Roman tradition of favouring brass and gunmetal. The use of brass for escutcheons for some bowls (where they exist), however, adds an interesting dimension to the discussion as it clearly indicates that brass was available when it was deemed appropriate, and often brass with a high zinc content suggesting that it was a primary product and therefore probably not re-cycled. Its use as an embellishment indicates that it was regarded as exotic, but this may only relate to the golden colour of the alloy and not to any particular problem in procurement. The metalworking tradition that was responsible for the hanging bowls therefore appears to have been highly selective in its choice of alloy and displays a different aesthetic to that of its neighbours. There seems to be a desire for relatively pure metals that were kept separate and used together to form decorative colour contrasts that must have contributed to these hanging bowls being regarded as highly prized items (Brenan 1991, 137). This aspect of the Wollaston bowl, evidenced by the indications of repair and a long working life, is also found in some of the other bowls published. The Wollaston bowl is also consistent with the other hanging bowls that have been studied scientifically in terms of its method of manufacture. The microstructures show that the bowl was raised from a single sheet of bronze with considerable technical skill involving multiple cycles of annealing and is therefore entirely consistent with the only other hanging bowls to have been examined in the same way, the bowls from Sutton Hoo.

The sword
by Ian Meadows

The sword is 880mm long, of which 100mm is the tang the remainder comprised a double-edged blade 30-35mm wide (Fig 3.19). Adhering to the blade are mineral replaced traces of the scabbard (see J Watson below) indicating the sword had been buried sheathed, no trace of either a chape or locket was found suggesting quite a plain scabbard (Bone 1989, 68). The sword was stereo X-rayed at the British Museum by Janet Lang and the description of the blade is partly from these radiographs.

The tang preserves traces of the grip and lower guard both of which were made from horn (see J Watson below) The size and form of the grip cannot be assessed but the lower guard was about 12mm thick and extended at least the width of the blade. The tang onto which these elements had fitted is 10mm wide at the end flaring to 16mm wide near the shoulder directly above the blade. On the radiograph a series of linear *striae* are apparent, they reflected the drawing together of the rods that lower down on the blade had been forged together in a pattern weld.

The blade flares from the tang and is divided into a series of decorative zones. The first zone 75mm long comprises a slightly sinuous area of pattern welding which at one stage prompted discussion about the Scandinavian practice of grinding the surface of pattern welded blades creating such an effect. The twisted bundles of rods, however, in this example are still clearly discernible so any grinding was only superficial. This zone gives way to a sequence of decorative zones in which the bundles with axes running down the line of the blade alternated across the blade, twisted, straight, twisted, straight, and also down the blade. This zone of pattern welding is consistently between 24-25mm across. The motif appears to be in two sections that repeat down the blade. The bundles occurring at 70, 80 and 75mm lengths and then 70, 80 and 75mm lengths again, beyond that point there are two further zones of four bundles measuring 75 and 70mm long above the final zone in which all the rods are drawn together tapering to an irregular point 8mm wide. Around the edge of the pattern-welded section there is a plain zone of metal about 9mm wide, this presumably was the cutting edge. It is unclear whether it was a different hardness than the rest of the sword. Although uncertain it would appear that there are on average four to five rods in each strip, although as Laing (1989, 91-2) points out, such estimates based only on radiographs are problematic.

Organic material associated with the sword
by Jacqui Watson

The iron sword is heavily corroded and the iron corrosion products have preserved a range of organic materials that were originally parts of the hilt and composite scabbard. These organic materials follow the pattern identified on other Saxon swords (Watson and Edwards 1990; Cameron 2000).

The nomenclature for the hilt follows Bone (1989). The sword tang is broken just below the position for the upper guard this means that there is only evidence for the grip and lower guard sections. Both of these sections are made from horn, which was easily recognisable with the aid of a hand lens. In the case of the grip the horn is aligned parallel with the axis of the tang. In the broken section a tiny wooden wedge is visible, but too small to sample for identification. Small slivers of wood were often used to fill any void between the iron tang and organic handle, and help hold the handle firmly in place.

In contrast with the grip, the horn section making the lower guard has the grain aligned across the tang, which makes it easy to distinguish it as a separate piece. This section is just over 12mm thick, and extends over the top of the blade presumably to ensure that it does not slip during use.

Scabbard

The scabbard on this sword has a composite construction with traces of three layers along different parts of the blade. Next to the blade are the remains of an animal pelt, with the hairs directly onto the metal surface and across the width of the blade. On top of the flesh side of the animal skin are traces of the thin wooden stiffeners. These have a tangential surface, possibly with a lenticulate section (Cameron 2000) and were most probably carefully cut into shape with a draw-knife. The wood is not well enough preserved to identify species, but according to Cameron in her survey most are willow or poplar.

In a few areas there are also traces of the outer leather covering, which originally would have held together the whole construction. Little of this layer is preserved as it was protected from the corroding iron blade by the other two layers, so not enough remains to see if there was any kind of decoration on it. There are a few traces of a white layer on the leather that might have been paint, but are more likely to have precipitated on to the object during burial.

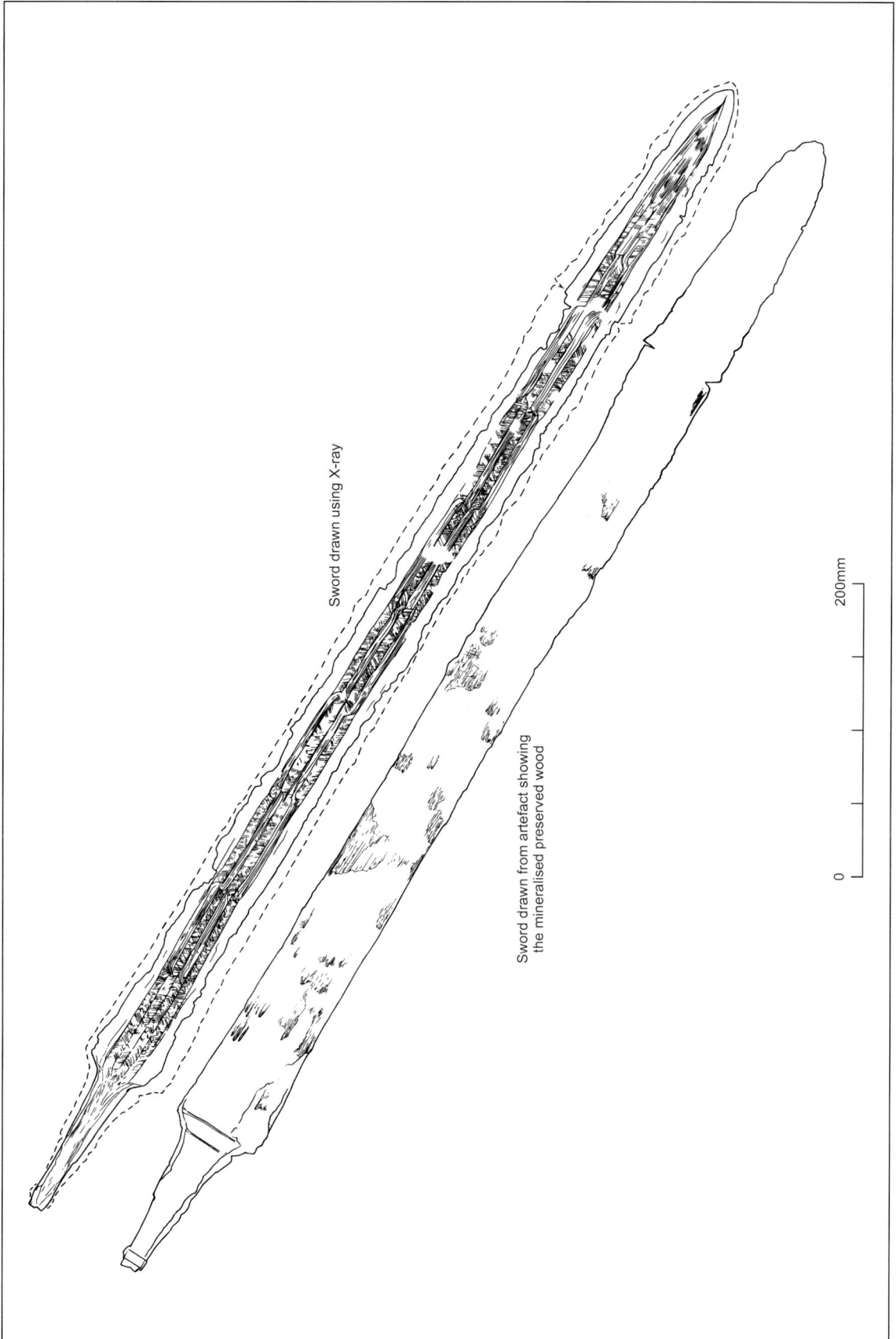

FIGURE 3.19. THE SWORD

Other artefacts
The knife, buckles, iron rods and clothing hook
by Ian Meadows

The knife

It is a simple iron knife blade 100mm long, 16mm broad (Fig 3.20). The back of the blade tapers about 16mm from its end and the tang does not survive. The size of the blade places it at the boundary between small and medium blades (Härke 1989).

The buckles

Buckle A (RA2)

Buckle A is a small iron buckle with iron plate (Fig 3.20). The oval frame is only 9mm wide and has an iron pin. The plate is 22mm long and tapered slightly from a maximum width of 10mm. At the narrow end a 5mm diameter rivet probably provided a fastening through leather or textile. As this small buckle is at the upper left shoulder it is likely to be a clothing buckle joining a small strap belt fastening.

Buckle C (RA3)

Buckle C comprised an iron buckle with a rectangular iron plate (Fig 3.20). The oval frame 19 x 9mm has a short centrally located pin. The plate is 14mm wide and 17mm long. The frame can accommodate straps up to 14mm wide. Two possible rivets were visible on the X-ray.

This buckle was located adjacent to the scabbard of the sword about 80mm below the shoulder of the blade. It was felt to probably be part of a suspension arrangement for the sword or perhaps part of some distributor strap

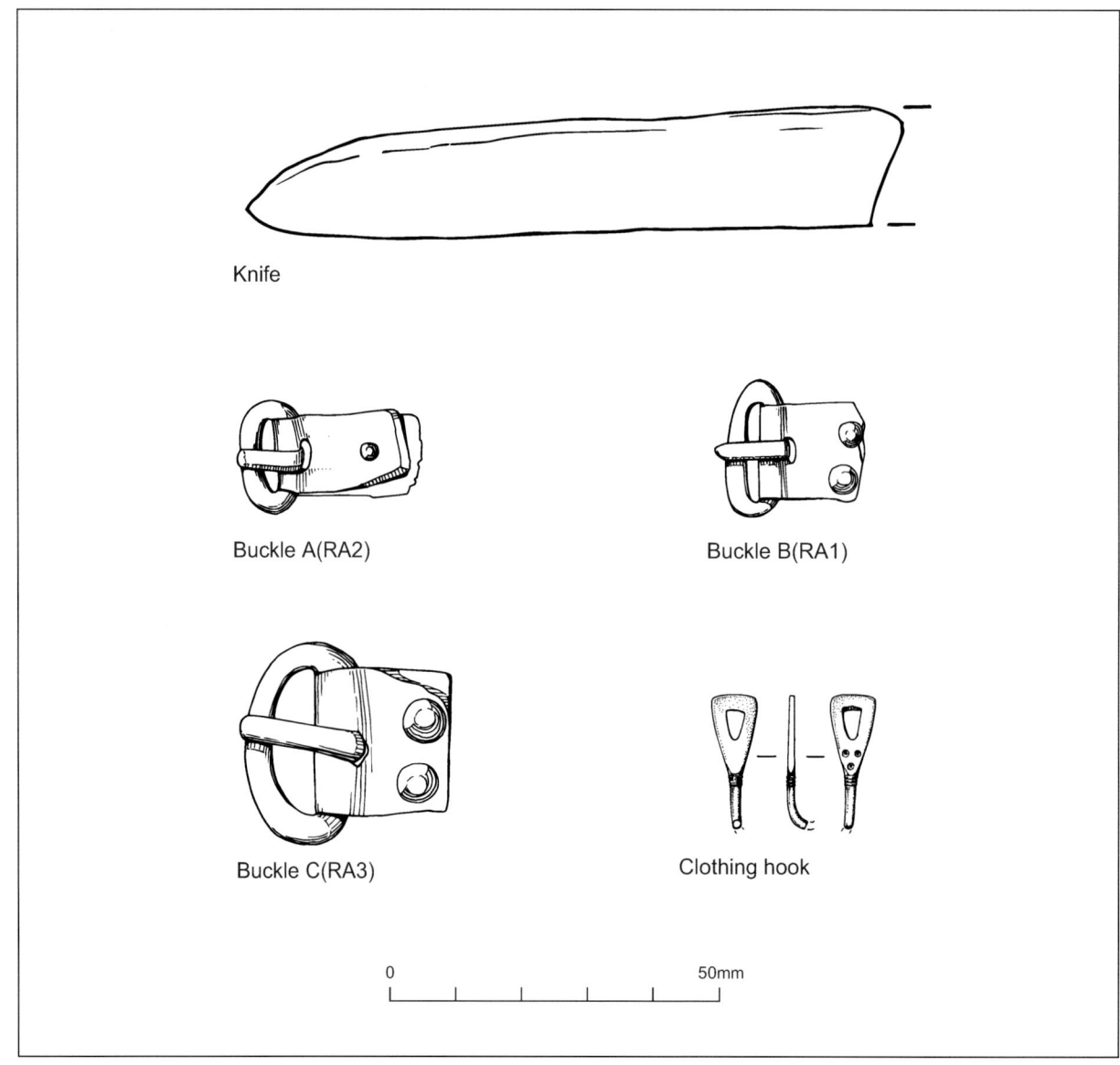

FIGURE 3.20. THE KNIFE, BUCKLES AND CLOTHING HOOK

arrangement. The sword from Westgarth grave 51 (West 1988) was placed in the grave unworn and although a stain suggested the sword belt had been about 25mm wide no buckles were found in association.

Buckle B (RA1)

Buckle B was an oval iron buckle with a wrapped around iron plate (Fig 3.20). The iron plate is 20mm long and tapered from 24 to 18mm wide. At its end two domed iron rivets/studs had attached it to the belt or strap. The oval frame could accommodate a strap 21mm wide.

The size of all three buckles is small and would fit in with a date in the later 7th century when belts narrow from the 20-30mm that was common in the 6th and early 7th centuries (Hirst 1985, 86). The buckles/plates represent variations of Marzinzik's (2003) type group 11.24b (307), a range of small oval buckles with rectangular or square plates attached. Marzinzik also dates this late form to the later 7th century AD.

The iron rods

A series of iron rods up to 30mm long were recovered from the plough drag material to the south of the helmet. These rods were originally considered as part of a neck guard or aventail composed of linked rods or a leather or textile example to which the rods may have been attached. The small number of rods would appear the render this suggestion untenable along with the absence of either a recognisable scatter outside the helmet or examples from within its fill.

The rods were also considered as possible belt stiffeners. Rod stiffeners can be seen from graves abroad, for example at Giengen grave 13 (Paulsen and Schach-Dörges 1978). It is possible therefore that they represent stiffeners to a belt, presumably ending in either buckle B or C.

A detailed examination of two groups of material (RA 4 & 5) containing rod elements was undertaken by A Draper, Royal Armouries in Leeds. It was found that the material was a mixture of iron fragments, lengths of solid iron rod 3-4mm diameter and hollow iron rods 3-4mm diameter. In the group RA5 four rods were preserved in a single block of corrosion and soil and they displayed similar characteristics of hollow round-sectioned shanks, broken at one end and flattened at the other. Additional fragments not part of the soil block included further flattened ends and lengths of tubular rods. The function of such iron tubes is hard to understand, as is their apparent association with the helmet or a belt or the reasons for their manufacture. It has been suggested that the tubes may have formed sockets for feather plumes or crests associated with the helmet but none were attached to the helmet.

The clothing hook

A cast copper alloy clothing hook was found which was 20mm long (Fig 3.20) comprising a small openwork triangular element with a circular sectioned hooked extension, the end of which is missing. The zone between the apex of the open triangle and the base of the hook arm is decorated with three ring/dot motifs, each about 0.75mm diameter. Further along the hook is a decorative bead/reel, beyond which the hook is plain. It is probable that stitching securing this piece to any clothing originally covered the plain part of the openwork triangle below the ring/dot motifs. Early hooks are known from several sites, for example Shakenoak (Dickinson 1973) and Winchester (Biddle 1990, 548), but none of the stratified published examples are of this form, most are solid triangular plates pierced by two holes for fixing.

Conservation report on the buckles
by Alison Draper

Introduction

Five small iron fragments from the burial were sent for conservation were given identification numbers, as they did not have individual finds numbers assigned:

RA1 – Buckle from shoulder area
RA2 – Buckle
RA3 – Buckle
RA4 – Miscellaneous fragments
RA5 – Plough deposits

Condition

The objects were covered in compacted sandy soil that incorporated many small stones.

Treatment

The objects were X-radiographed to establish what was present within each concretion (150 Kv, 5mA, 30 seconds). This also revealed the condition of the objects to be poor, with no metal remaining within the concretions. Investigation continued with hand tools and air abrasive cleaning under a microscope. Some of the objects showed evidence of mineral-preserved organic material and so were not cleaned further.

Descriptions

RA3, buckle C

X-radiography revealed this to be a buckle with a single-loop oval frame and a double plate (Fig 3.21). The iron pin is still present and protrudes beyond the frame. The plate is *c*15mm long and has two rivet holes evenly spaced at the end of the plate. Remains of the rivets were visible and they appear to be iron.

The Pioneer burial

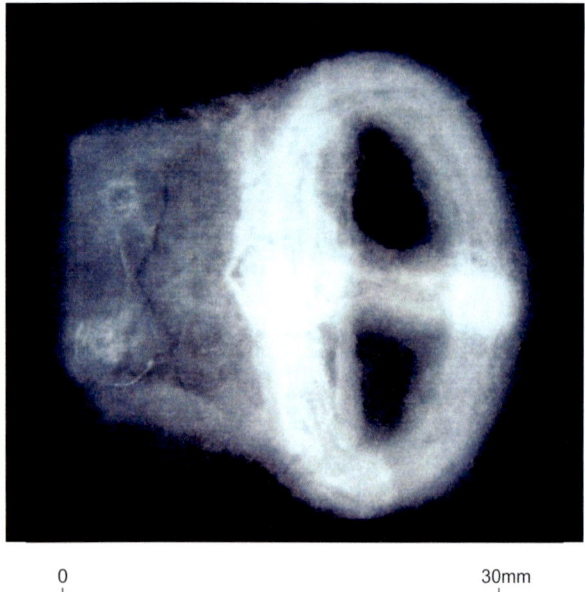

Figure 3.21. X-radiograph of RA3 (buckle C)

Figure 3.22. RA3 (buckle C), textile seen to left of black line

Investigative cleaning revealed the metal to be in a heavily corroded condition, with no original surface remaining. One side of the buckle has mineral preserved textile present (Figs 3.22 and 3.23). This was visible as both a woven area and as individual threads along the lower edge.

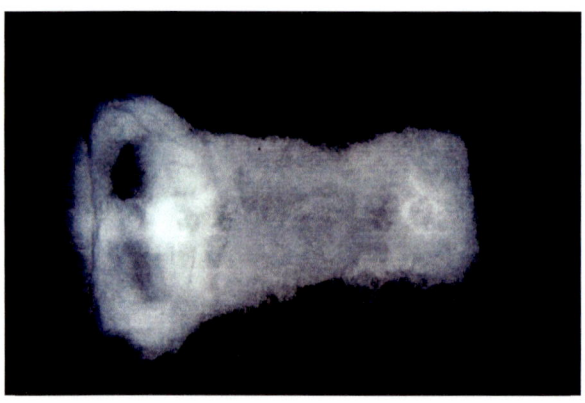

Figure 3.24. X-radiograph of RA2 (buckle A)

Figure 3.23. RA3 (buckle C), other side, semi-circular piece of metal can be seen

Figure 3.25. RA2 (buckle A), after cleaning, side 1

Figure 3.26. RA2 (buckle A), after cleaning, side 2

Chapter 3 Artefacts

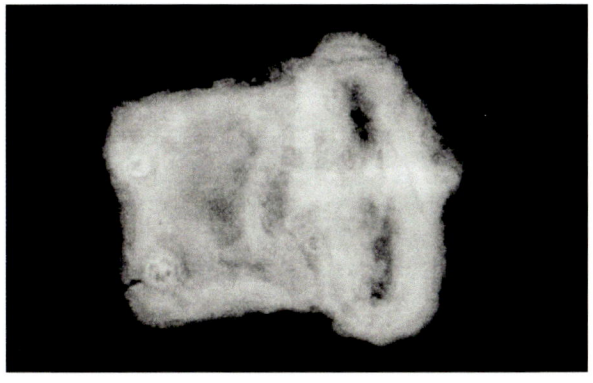

FIGURE 3.27. X-RADIOGRAPH OF RA1 (BUCKLE B)

RA1, buckle B

This object is clearly a buckle (buckle B), even when covered in soil deposits and corrosion products. Although no records were available, it appeared that some investigation by air abrasive cleaning had already occurred.

X-radiography revealed this to be a buckle with a single loop D-shaped frame and a double plate (Fig 3.27). There are two evenly spaced rivet holes on the end of the plate. The rivet holes have both the remains of rivets present as well as clearly defined circular washers. The washers have a radio-opaque material round their edge, suggesting that they may be plated by a material more dense than iron. The washers and the rivets appear to be iron. There is a V-shaped feature around the loop of the pin. The plate is c19mm long by 19mm wide, and the D-shaped loop is c30mm wide (Figs 3.28 and 3.29).

RA1, side 2

This side of the buckle has extensive mineral-preserved organic remains. This is visible around the loop where a smooth compact layer may once have been leather. There are also extensive textile remains on the lower half of the plate, shown both as woven areas and individual threads. The relationship between the leather and the textile is not clear.

RA4, described as miscellaneous fragments

When X-radiographed, they resembled the fragments found in RA5 (see below).

RA4, A-F

A – flat piece of iron

RA4

B – hollow tube with round section, 25mm long, 4mm diameter

FIGURE 3.28. RA1 (BUCKLE B), SIDE 1

FIGURE 3.29. RA1 (BUCKLE B), SIDE 2

RA2, buckle A

Described as an iron fitting, X-radiography revealed RA2 to be a buckle (buckle A). It is a single loop oval-framed buckle with a double plate. This possibly has mineral-preserved organic material between the two plates. X-radiography shows a single central rivet at the end of the plate. The plate is c20mm long by 11mm wide. The frame is c18mm wide (Figs 3.24 and 3.25).

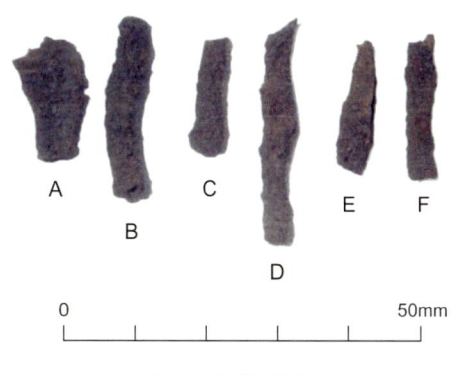

FIGURE 3.30. RA4

C – length of iron with round section, 15mm long, 3mm diameter

D – length of iron with round section, 32mm long, 3mm diameter

E – broken length of iron with round section, possibly hollow, 12mm long, 4mm diameter

F – length of iron with round section, 20mm long, 4mm diameter

RA5, described as plough deposits

There were five possible objects contained in one soil block (Fig 3.31). Investigation by mechanical methods, pin vice and air abrasive, revealed four objects with long shanks of a round section. These shanks appear to be of a hollow tubular construction as there is no metal or magnetite remaining in the centre. The centre of the shank also contains a different sort of iron corrosion product of a pale orange very fine powder, which was only seen in possible voids and areas where two different pieces of iron met. The objects themselves were in a very poor and corroded condition. There is no metal left within and the original surface is incoherent and difficult to identify under the microscope.

All four pieces appear to have a similar construction. They have shanks of round section, which appear to be hollow tubes. All four of these examples have one end missing and this conforms to the limits of the soil block (see X-ray; Fig 3.31). The other ends of these objects are all similar in that it is a deliberately-formed, flattened and rounded shape. All pieces also showed evidence of a circular iron feature on one side of the rounded 'head' (Fig 3.32). The opposite side to this is flat, with no sign of any shank or metal piercing this rounded end (Fig 3.33).

The first object:

1: is 34mm long and has a split in the top. This may have been a split in the metal object or it could be a result of corrosion.

2: has the best-preserved rounded head, which clearly shows the circular feature on one side. The diameter of this circular feature is 6mm; the opposite side is flat and relatively smooth. The total length 24mm.

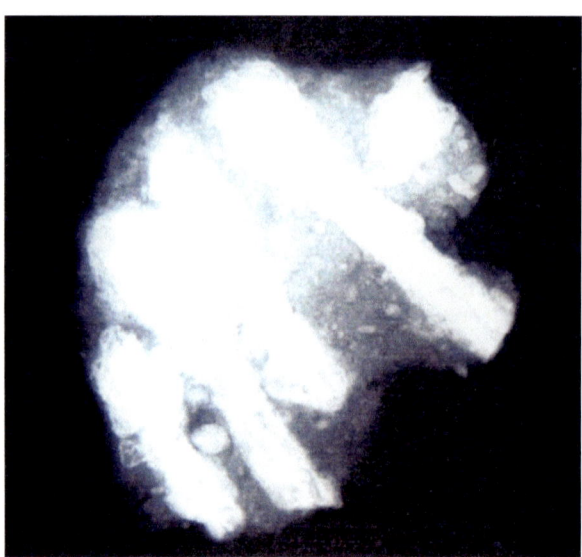

FIGURE 3.31. RA5 A, X-RADIOGRAPH OF SOIL BLOCK

3: has a distorted, twisted shank with corrosion products on the broken end that prevented identification as a hollow tube. The other end is rounded with the remains of the circular feature found on the other examples. Total length 30mm.

4: was heavily corroded but still retains evidence of a rounded end with a circular feature in the centre. There is another possible piece of metal twisting round the shank but corrosion made identification difficult. Total length 24mm.

5: fragments, only shown on X-ray. One has a circular cross-section and may have been part of a shank and measures 14mm long. The other fragment may have been part of a rounded head seen on the other objects, or was possibly a rivet, as a flattened circular area is visible at each end. Between these two circular areas, there are possibly the remains of mineral-preserved organic material, although these were not diagnostic in any way.

FIGURE 3.32. RA5 GROUP A FROM SOIL BLOCK (SIDE WITH CIRCULAR FEATURE)

RA5, individual fragments B-D (Fig 3.33).

B: hollow tube of round section. 4mm diameter, 10mm maximum length

C: two lengths with round cross sections. The longest has a diameter of 4mm and is 14mm long. The smaller one has a diameter of 3mm and is 7mm long.

Chapter 3 Artefacts

FIGURE 3.33. RA5, INDIVIDUAL FRAGMENTS B-E

D: one length of iron with circular cross section 3mm in diameter and 8mm long.

E: two fragments, one is flattened with a rounded end and circular feature, similar to the objects found in RA5-A soil block. There is evidence of it originally having a hollow shank. The second fragment consists of two hollow tubes of circular section, which have corroded together. One has evidence of the tube widening out into the typical rounded end seen on the other examples.

B and C appear to be fragments of the same object type as seen in the soil block.

Textiles remains possibly relating to bedding
by Penelope Walton-Rogers

Introduction

Traces of textile have been found on the outside of the helmet, on the left-hand side, which was the side that faced downwards in the burial (Fig 3.34). There are two different textiles present, one a simple tabby weave (A), which is mainly towards the crown of the helmet, and the other a patterned weave (B), lower down and towards the back. Both textiles are poorly preserved and heavily mineralised. Scanning-electron microscopy (by P Clogg, University of Durham) and transmitted-light microscopy (by the author) failed to produce firm identification of the fibres, although the fine, smooth fibres of textile A suggest flax (linen) and the mixed diameters of textile B suggest wool.

Textile A

The tabby-weave textile A (Fig 3.35a), has survived in patches, the largest of which is 30 x 30mm. It has been woven with Z-spun yarn in warp and weft, with 10 x 10 threads per 10mm. In one area the count is higher at 16 x 10 threads per 10mm: this may represent the edge of the fabric, as warp threads tend to bunch at the selvedges.

If it is correct to identify this as linen, then it is an unusually coarse example. Linen tabbies are common in early Saxon cemeteries, but those used for clothing generally have between 14 and 22 threads per 10mm.

FIGURE 3.34. DETAIL OF TEXTILES

This, then, may be a piece of canvas, coarse sheeting or perhaps a mattress cover.

Textile B

Textile B seems to be a pattern weave of some sort, although it is too poorly preserved for full details to be recorded. It covers an area 150 x 60mm, the best patches being 25 x 20mm. It consists of a ground weave with z-spun yarn in warp and weft and a pattern made from floating threads of thicker S-spun yarn. The S-spun threads all run in the same direction and in the best preserved area they form a loose brick-work pattern (Fig 3.35b). One S-spun pattern thread alternates with one Z-spun thread of the ground weave. There are approximately 7 Z-spun and 7 S-spun per 10mm (14 threads per 10mm in all), but it has not been possible to count the threads per cm in the crossways system and the identity of the ground weave is not known.

This was originally thought to be the reverse face of a pile weave, the tufted pile having faced towards the helmet. The spacing and arrangement of the supposed pile threads, however, is not an exact match for any of the pile weaves recorded so far. It more closely resembles a pattern weave found in Alamannic row-grave cemeteries of the Frankish controlled southern Germany, known as *Wolltuch mit Musterkette*, 'wool cloth with pattern warp'(Hundt 1966,

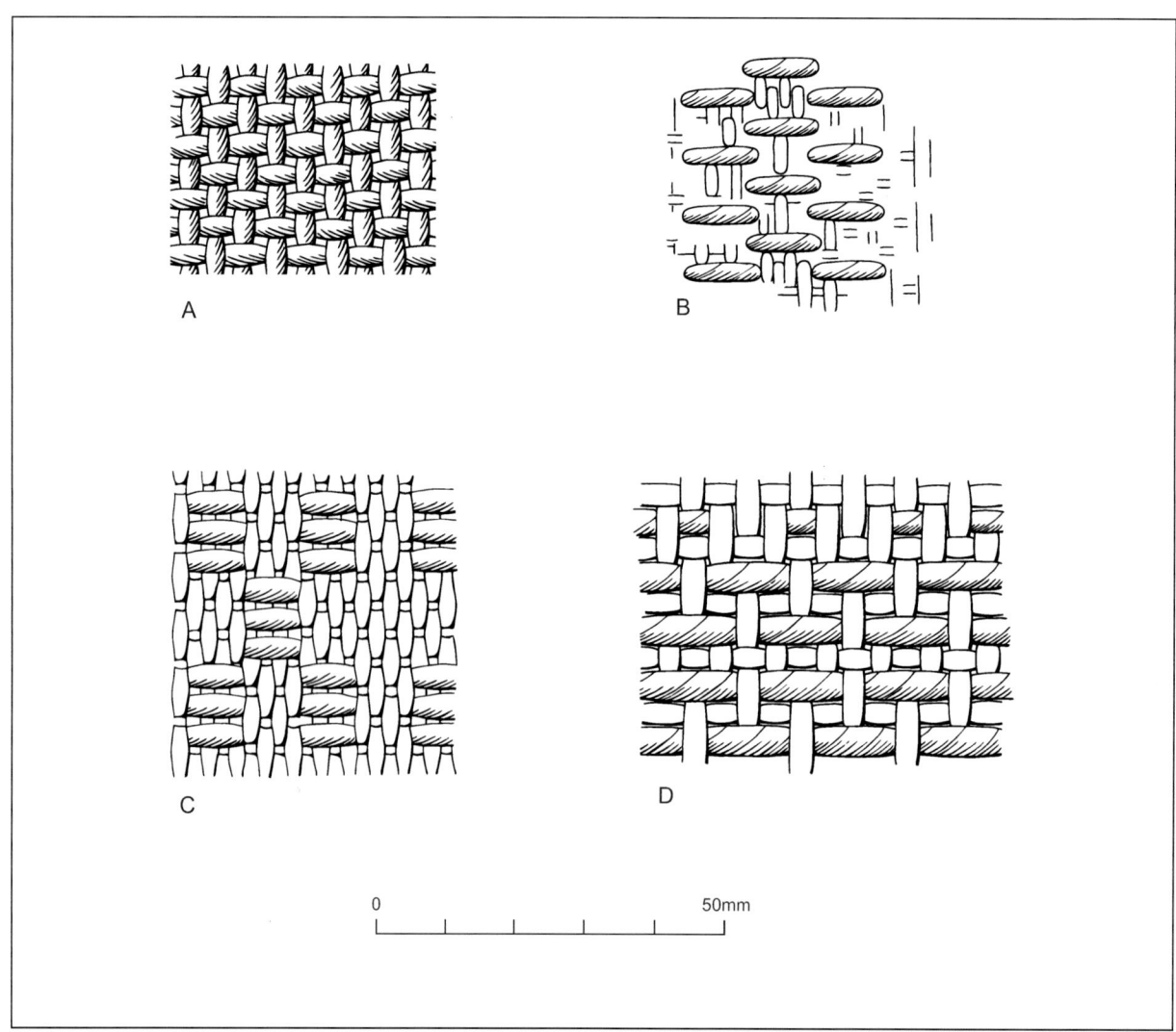

FIGURE 3.35. TEXTILES

1972, 1978: Bender Jørgensen 1986, 356, 1992, 145-7). In this, a ground weave of Z x Z tabby is combined with thick, softly spun Z or S pattern threads, the pattern threads alternating with single threads of the ground weave (Fig 3.19c), as in the Wollaston example; indeed, one example from Giengen an der Brenz, Kries Heidenheim (Grave 26, Hundt 1978, 152-3, 156-7, 161), has the same thread count and yarn combination as the Wollaston piece. On the other hand, in the German examples, the design is built up in units of three pattern threads (Fig 3.35c), whereas the Wollaston example belongs to the same general group as the German pattern weaves, it is not necessarily Alamannic or Frankish in origin.

These weaves have reversible patterns made up of simple geometric motifs. The pattern threads are probably a different colour from the ground weave, so that the design on the back is a negative of the front. Although no examples of the 'wool cloth with pattern warp' have been previously recorded in England, there is another Saxon textile which has similar characteristics. This is known as 'summer-and-winter', which is also reversible and has geometric designs (Fig 3.35d). 'Summer-and-Winter' has a more complicated structure than the Wollaston weave, but the pattern is again produced by alternating threads, one ground (Z-spun) and one patterned (Z-or S-spun). Three examples of this weave have been recorded so far, one from Wakerley, not far from Wollaston (Grave 85, Crowfoot 1988), and others from Mucking, Essex (Grave 939, Crowfoot unpublished), and Market Lavington, Wilts (Grave 23, Walton-Rogers 2006).

'Summer-and-winter' is generally regarded as a coverlet weave and the examples from Wakerley and Mucking had been used to cover the body and the grave goods. Function of the German pattern weaves is not known.

Most come from well-furnished men's graves and have been found in the vicinity of the waist and hips- although this may reflect a clustering of iron artifacts in that area. It may be significant that the two graves with these pattern weaves at Giengen an der Brenz both had remains of feather pillows near the head (Hundt 1978, 162). The angle of the head in the Wollaston grave also suggested the presence of a pillow or some other head support (Meadows op.cit. 392).

Conclusion

Although it is impossible to identify textile B with certainty, the circumstantial evidence suggests that it is part of a patterned coverlet placed under the body and the helmet. A pillow at the head would complete the picture of a body laid out as if on a bed or couch. The role of the coarse linen, textile A, is not known, but it may have been an undersheet, or perhaps a mattress cover.

Chapter 4

Human remains

Skeletal report
by Jenny Wakely
with note on dental remains by J N James

The skeletal remains were fragmentary and in poor condition. Fragments of skull and leg bones and some teeth were present which could give some very general information about the individual. Because of the fragility of the material, cleaning was only attempted on the largest pieces.

The skull

The remains consist of fragments from the back and side of the skull, some of which showed the full thickness of the bone but others consisted of inner or outer table only. Several fragments bore a green staining presumably derived from proximity to the hanging bowl. Few anatomically recognisable features could be seen, and the fragments could not be reconstructed because of their fragility.

The identified pieces comprised a piece of mastoid process, too small to determine sex or side identification, part of the back of the parietal bones including a length of the sagittal suture and the impression of an arachnoid granulation. The suture was closed externally but open internally, indicating an individual who had not reached middle age. Fragments from the squamous part of the occipital bone, which, by their thickness and curvature and lack of strong muscle markings, appear to have come from a lightly built person without heavy muscle development in the neck.

No pathological features could be identified because of poor preservation.

The legs

The right femur was represented by a mid/lower shaft fragment 114mm long in a poor state of preservation and assorted small fragments. The thickness of the bone and the slight development of the muscle attachment (linea aspera) on the back of the femur indicated an adult of slender build and slight muscle development. The left leg was represented by small fragments some of which could be identified as pieces of the shaft of a femur.

No pathological changes could be detected and no features diagnostic of age or sex have been preserved.

The dentition

Parts of 15 teeth, all loose, were present (Upper Right 8, 7, 6, 5 and 4: Lower Right 8, 7, 6, 5, 4, 3 and 2 : Lower Left 8, 7 and 3). There was considerable taphonomic change in the teeth. Much dentine had been destroyed and there was macroscopic evidence for some enamel porosity. The following teeth were represented by their crowns only - Upper Right 7, 6, 5 and 4; Lower Right 5 and 2; Lower Left 3. The remaining teeth all had roots present but none was complete and all apices were missing.

There was no evidence of dental caries. The distal surface of the LR 6 was missing and so cannot be examined. No hypoplasia was seen. No calculus was present. It was possible to occlude the upper and lower premolars and molars, which revealed a normal relationship of the upper and lower teeth. Five teeth had attrition classified by Brothwell's method as follows;-UR7 2+,UR6 2+, LR7 2+, LR 6 3+ and LL7 2 (Brothwell 1972, 69)

The attrition suggests an age towards the higher end of the range 17-25. The absence of the root apices and the poor state of preservation of the dentine preclude age estimation by sectioning.

Summary

The remains were fragmentary and poorly preserved. They represented the body of a lightly built young adult, probably less than 25 years of age. The absence of hypoplasia suggested that he did not suffer any severe illnesses or periods of malnutrition during his childhood, tentatively suggesting membership of a privileged social group in his community by right of birth. The absence of dental caries is typical of individuals taking a diet low in refined carbohydrate.

Chapter 5

Discussion

By Rob Atkins and Ian Meadows

Overview

The Pioneer burial comprised the remains of a young adult male in his 20s who was buried at around the end of the 7th century AD with significant grave goods. This burial was dated and sexed through the associated/accompanying artefacts, which consisted of a boar-crested iron helmet, a sword, hanging bowl, knife, clothing hook and three iron buckles from clothing or straps (Fig 5.1). He was placed in the grave with objects either of significance for their rarity and status or the quality of workmanship. No spearheads or shield boss was recovered from the grave but these artefacts generally occur high in grave fills and as this grave only survived to a depth of 0.15m such pieces may have been lost to later ploughing of the site.

The particular grave goods with this burial set the Pioneer grave aside from nearly all other interments of the early to middle Saxon period in the country. The presence of not only the helmet but also the pattern-welded sword and hanging bowl strongly suggest he had been an Anglian warrior of high status, possibly even as high as of æðeling class (man of royal blood i.e. a nobleman). His burial location, probably under a mound, had also been placed at a significant geographical position (see below) and these indirect factors may also suggest he had perhaps been a landowner on this area.

The location for the Pioneer burial was important and this ties in with Saxon cemeteries which are also sometimes placed in discrete locations. These may have been the product of cultural choice with their continued use reflecting social custom. The siting of a single significant burial, not constrained by a cemetery, clearly would be the result of more complex factors than simply the disposal of a body. The main purposes of a grave are normally seen as being a vessel for allowing the transition of a spirit into the afterlife, containing the earthly remains safely and also as a memorial. The continued existence of a person as a memory is achieved through the continued presence in this world of visual stimulae; a burial monument is one such visible feature. The burial was therefore positioned at a location that would have ensured a level of continued remembrance next to a routeway by the River Nene. In death the remains have been sited where they would have the effect of reinforcing the control and presence of an elite by being visible beside these routes.

Direct parallels with the Pioneer burial are few, but there are similarities between high status warrior burials in the type of grave goods recovered and where they were buried to suggest 'important' men were buried in a certain distinct way and this can be seen in certain details recorded in Saxon poems such as Beowulf. The rarity of the Pioneer burial can be seen in how few helmets (or parts of helmets) have been found in England from the post-Roman period to the Norman Conquest (Fig 5.2; including Staffordshire Hoard fragments).

The location of the Pioneer burial

The discovery of a rich 'princely' burial at Wollaston was unexpected owing to the almost complete absence of evidence for contemporary (and earlier) Saxon activity from the immediate study area. Early Saxon occupation dating up to the early 7th century was located on higher ground a little over 1.5km to the east (Chapman and Jackson 1992). The present village of Wollaston 2km to the east of the Pioneer burial has produced the remains of a notable middle and late Saxon settlement at Dando Close and other locations (Semmelmann and Ashworth 2004; Hall 1977).

The area of archaeological study within the quarries produced only isolated finds of early to middle Saxon material and comprised either stray pottery sherds within the ploughsoil or isolated brooch fragments. In contrast this area had been fairly densely occupied in pre-Saxon times, with continuous activity from the middle Iron Age until the late Roman period. The presumption is that the site had become marginal and/or used for agriculture during the post-Roman period. Saxon burials elsewhere are sometimes located in an area where there were significant prehistoric monuments but in this case at Wollaston the nearest Bronze Age and Neolithic funerary monuments were located about 0.5km to the south of the Pioneer burial on a slight ridge (See Chapter 1).

Routeways in relation to the Pioneer burial

Throughout the Iron Age and Roman periods a routeway aligned north-east to south-west ran through the quarry. The location of this route was close to the limits of the spread of medieval (and presumably earlier) alluviation, perhaps reflecting a position that in earlier times had also been beyond the winter flood limit. In addition to the main road route the excavations at Wollaston quarry found that a series of secondary routes were present in the Roman field system presumably linking farms to the main route. The Pioneer burial was placed 8m to the east of the main route and 220m to the south of a side

The Pioneer burial

FIGURE 5.1. HELMET, HANGING BOWL AND PATTERN-WELDED SWORD

road and 120m to the north of a crossroads. There was no evidence for the continued usage of the Roman farms along the route which did appear to have been abandoned, as no early Saxon finds were recovered from any of them (Meadows and Atkins forthcoming). The discovery of this burial beside this road would however suggest its continued usage into this period. The subsequent open field system, however, lay on a different alignment to the tracks suggesting that by the late Saxon period this communication network had been abandoned: - it is uncertain how soon after the interment of the Pioneer burial this abandonment occurred.

CHAPTER 5 DISCUSSION

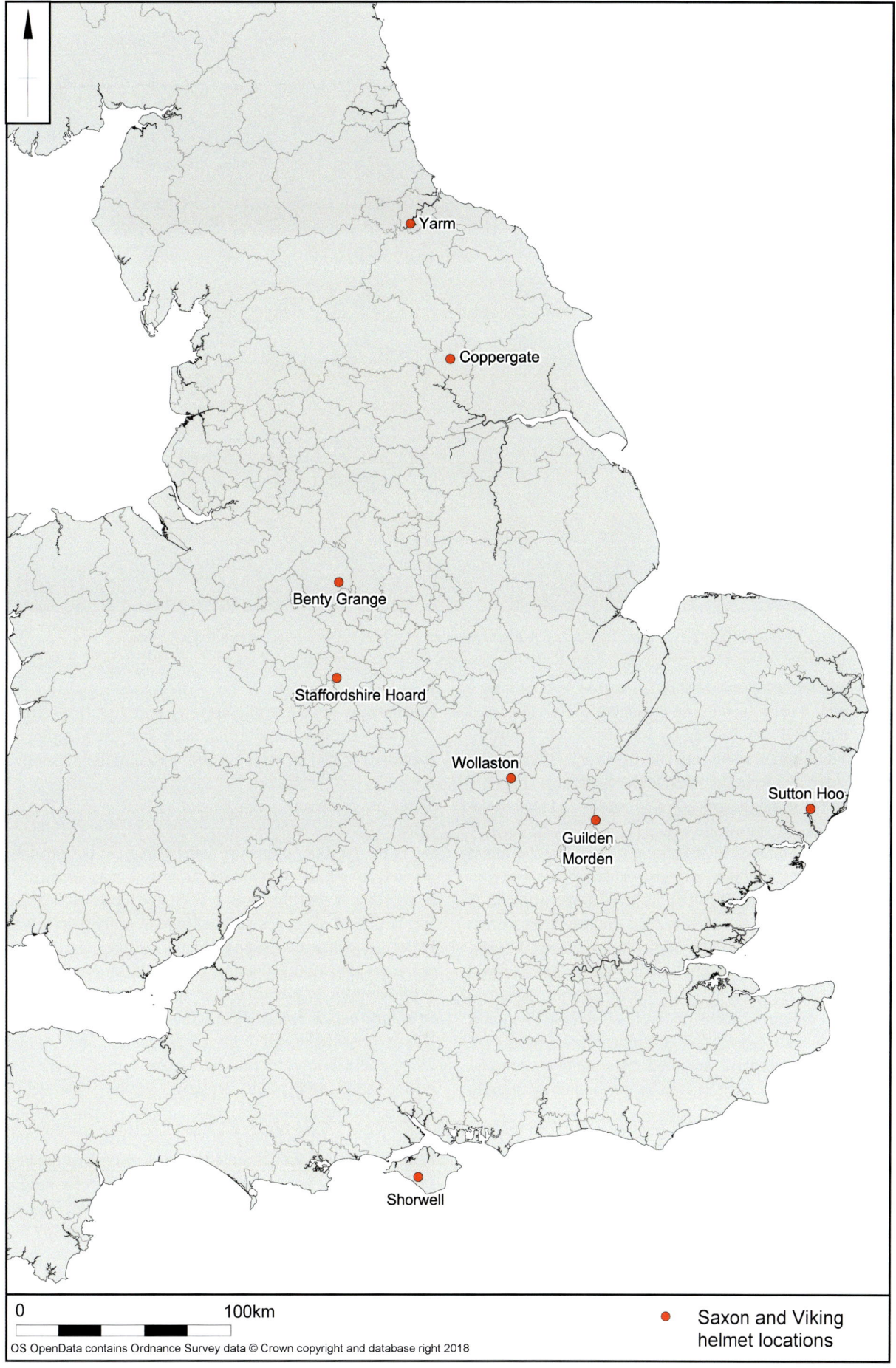

FIGURE 5.2. PIONEER BURIAL IN ITS NATIONAL SETTING WITH OTHER SAXON (AND VIKING) HELMETS LOCATED

THE PIONEER BURIAL

FIGURE 5.3. VIEW ALONG THE LINE OF THE ROMAN ROAD TO THE PIONEER BURIAL, LOOKING SOUTH-WEST

This main route was established in the Iron Age initially a drove which continued in use through the Roman period when part of it was flanked by side ditches. It probably formed the Roman route between Towcester, 25km to the south-west, and Irchester, 5km to the north-east (Figs 1.1 and 5.3). By siting the grave beside a route and near to the other routes, the burial site would presumably be seen by a substantial number of people, ensuring the continued memory of the deceased and also allowing the grave to act as a societal marker. The issue of remembrance is likely therefore to have influenced the selection of this location for the burial. This individual required a burial that reflected his status but equally that status required his burial to be sited in a prominent location ensuring continued memory. The wide flat floodplain at this point would have contained few prominent landmarks, the Roman field boundaries and roads presumably continued to be marked into the post Roman period but essentially this is a flat area of land.

O'Brien suggests that some warrior burials including the Pioneer burial at Wollaston may have been guarding routeways and boundaries (O'Brien 1999, 100). O'Brien stated that in the middle Anglia area (which includes Northamptonshire) warrior burials were not unusual and that some of these isolated discrete warrior burials, including the Pioneer burial, might be regarded as sentinel including eight isolated burials distributed along the line of and near to the Icknield Way. This was a clearly defined border between the territory of the middle Angles and that of the East Saxons suggesting the Saxons may have been perceived as a threat (*ibid*, 100). This would mean these burials were not just a continued memory but had an ongoing active role in the present.

There are numerous examples of early to middle Saxon cemeteries respecting Roman roads in the East Midlands in both Northamptonshire (including Peterborough) as well as adjacent counties such as Leicestershire. It is significant that this was a frequent location selected for burial of all types (cremation or inhumation) and beliefs (pagan or Christian) which took place throughout the early and middle Saxon period. Examples include a 6th century pagan mixed cremation and inhumation cemetery which respected a Roman road 3km west of Botolph Bridge, Peterborough (Spoerry and Atkins 2015, 129). Early to middle Saxon burials were cut into a late Neolithic/early Bronze Age burial mound at Tansor, Northamptonshire, which may have stood beside a precursor of a medieval road that may have dated to the Roman period as well as an adjacent windmill of the late 12th century (Chapman 1997). At Castor, Peterborough, a late 6th-century cemetery was aligned on the Roman road at King Street despite the fact the surface of the Roman road was no longer extant but the route may still have functioned and been respected (Taylor and Angus 1999, 95-97). At Kibworth, Leicestershire there was a small open-ground middle Saxon Christian inhumation burial ground dating to the late 7th to 8th centuries adjacent to a Roman road (Shipley and Finn

2018). The presence of a medieval headland along the trackway at Kibworth may further support the idea that the trackway left a visual or topographic marker to the landscape well into the medieval period. In Derbyshire, secondary burials in prehistoric barrows and new 7th-century barrows were constructed along the line of the Derby to Buxton Roman road (Vince 2006, 172). The burial practice of location next to roads in rural areas away from settlements does not seem to take place after the late 7th or 8th century and the Pioneer burial was therefore a late example of this practice.

The River Nene and land boundaries

The grave was possibly aligned perpendicular to a contemporary course of the River Nene so (assuming the channel hasn't moved too far) the warrior burial would possibly be facing it to the north-west- north direction. The grave was on slightly higher ground which had been ploughed since at least the medieval period. It lay to the south-east and overlooking the floodplain/ partly floodplain land areas. The latter was called *Ryholme* which had anciently been partly ploughed and partly meadow area, and surrounded by brooks (Hall 1977, fig 1). On slightly lower land to the north-west of *Ryholme* were the extensive floodplain and the River Nene channels themselves.

The Pioneer burial was adjacent to the south-western corner of the Higham Hundred boundary where it meets the River Nene. The River Nene and Roman road location was important (even if the river was not navigable). It was similar in both regards to a site at Asthall, North Oxfordshire where a burial mound overlooked Akeman Street, immediately above an abandoned Roman settlement that straddled the road where it crossed the River Windrush (Williams 1999). There are similarities between the Wollaston burial and elements of the late Saxon poem describing Beowulf's burial where a mound was raised over his tomb where it was visible to seafarers and was hung about with helmets. This Saxon tradition had not been unusual in Roman Britain when burial clubs would recall the names of dead members at gatherings and rich individuals would erect either substantial grave monuments, for example Bartlow Hills, Cambridgeshire (Gage 1834). There were examples of people erecting monuments away from the burial as memorials, for example the Igel pillar from near Trier in Germany, erected at a road junction, which celebrates a rich cloth making family. In the later Viking period, an account of a Rus cremation, observed by Ibn Fadlan, was followed by the erection of a small earthen mound on which a post with the deceased's name was written (Jones 1968).

The association between boundaries and burials may need to be taken with caution and tempered. Vince (2006, 170) has pointed out that whilst studies appear to show a tendency for Saxon cemeteries to occur more often than chance would allow on or close to parish boundaries they make the assumption that land divisions in the 10th to 12th centuries, when parish boundaries were being fixed, are relevant to the 5th- to 7th-century social landscape. Brown *et al* were more certain in their opinion on this and thought that Northamptonshire estate boundaries were fixed by the 6th or 7th centuries when burials were being interred and probably date sometime in the Roman period to the early centuries of Saxon England (Brown *et al* 1977, 172).

The boundary of the later Wollaston parish with Strixton parish was also at this point, and here a newly planted marker in the *c*12th century was called *Longhedge* (Hall 1977, 23 and fig 1; See Chapter 1). Some Saxon cemeteries such as Wakerley lie on township boundaries but this may be a random association. Two Saxon charters refer to heathen burials on bounds, at Badby (Brown *et al* 1977, 156 points 21 and 22 and fig 3) and Newnham (quoted in Brown *et al* 1977, 172). Grinsell in his study of barrows noted that Saxons used heathen burials to mark the boundaries of estates most of which survive as our present parishes and thought that barrows largely pre-dated the use of boundaries (Grinsell 1991, 51). Brown *et al* (*1977*, 172) in contrast to Grinsell saw that burials may have post-dated the boundaries. They thought that the regularity of pagan Saxon burials sited on or very close to parish boundaries implied it, "was a deliberate act on the part of those responsible for the burials and that the boundaries so used were already in existence defining estates and may well have been doing so for centuries." Other examples of this phenomenon in the county include burials at Norton and Borough Hill, Daventry (Brown *et al* 1977, 172). Foard thought the potentially most significant example of association between burial and boundaries was the high status Pioneer burial which lay very close to Wollaston township boundary, which may also have been the boundary of the eight Hundreds of Oundle (Foard 1999, 12).

Burial time period

The Wollaston burial seems to have been deliberately placed at this location and from the blow-fly pupae cases preserved in the corrosion-products on the inside of the helmet, it is clear that he did not die in winter and that there had been some delay between his death and burial. As he could have been taken to other places after his death, the location of the Wollaston site for the burial was probably of some importance to him and/or the people who buried him. Presumably the burial ceremony would have been planned over several days, with people able to take part in the ceremony and to see him with grave goods displayed reflecting his status (see below).

Delay in burial has been seen elsewhere with the remains of insects in burials used to suggest that the dead in early Saxon England were not interred immediately, but were left within structures or in the grave where they could be viewed (Williams 2006, 124). This practice of burial sometime after death seems to have happened on 'simple' burials as well as to the very wealthy such as at Wollaston and in cemeteries of all sizes. Williams quotes evidence from the large cemetery at Snape (and elsewhere) referring to mineralised fly pupae but states the precise length between death and burial and the manner of exposure of the dead remain unclear (*ibid*, 124). This practice of 'late' burial after death has been recorded in two other Saxon cemeteries in Northamptonshire. At the 6th to early 7th century cemetery at Wakerley, which contained 85 graves, there were remains of empty pupae cases, replaced by corrosion on iron or bronze objects from some of the graves (Adams and Jackson 1989, 78). At Bozeat Quarry, only a few kilometres from the Wollaston site, within a small Saxon cemetery of five graves which dated to the late 6th to 7th centuries an example was found in an adult burial [741] with insect lava casings still attached to an iron buckle (Atkins 2018, 66-67 and especially fig 3.19).

Wollaston in relation to Saxon administrative organisation

Any attempt to understand the landscape around Wollaston in the middle Saxon period needs to examine/explore both the archaeological evidence and the problems of written sources. A Roman villa, of which the bath house was examined, lay directly to the west of Wollaston and 1.5km east from the Pioneer burial (Chapman and Jackson 1992). Foard himself noted (1985, 210) that, "one should look to the Saxon estate centres and seigneuril residences for a direct relationship with underlying or immediately adjacent villas." The questions of possible continuity from Roman villas to Saxon estates have been extensively argued with differences of opinions expressed. At Higham Ferrers, for example, the excavators argued that the Roman villa had probably been deserted and cleared with the Saxon incomers just opportunistic to settle at this location and the fact the area became an estate centre was a coincidence (Hardy *et al* 2007, 185-6). Other possibilities of continuity of estates have been suggested at Rothley, Leicestershire where there was a Roman villa and a Saxon estate centre with minster church in the same location (Upson-Smith 2016). Hardy *et al* (2007, 186) postulate that, "as the available database of sites and evidence has accumulated in the last few decades, the reality begins to look less uniform than earlier scenaros would have it, and researchers seem to be moving perhaps reluctantly towards the conclusion that the transition process was more influenced by small-scale circumstance, the personalities of the incomers, and the reception accorded them by the native population."

The significant middle Saxon settlement of Higham Ferrers lay less than 20km to the north-east of Wollaston and the later Hundred was named after Higham Ferrers (Wollaston was also within this Hundred; Fig 1.1). In Higham there was a large oval enclosure of middle Saxon date associated with the high status settlement (Hardy *et al* 2007). It was an estate centre but the size and extent of this estate is unknown with the excavation evidence showing it dated to phase 2 - about the late 7th to early 8th century (Foard 1999, 2; Foard 1985, fig 1; Hardy *et al* 2007, including 193). If this was the case, then Pioneer burial may have been contemporary with the period Higham was an estate centre, and if so the suggested Wollaston estate may have been at least secondary to Higham? Unfortunately some landholdings fragmented during the middle and late Saxon period which had meant that estate centres largely did not survive to the Domesday Book. Because of the paucity of the survival of Saxon records in Northamptonshire few estate centres are known (Hardy *et al* 2007, 191). A rare example which shows what probably occurred in the county is the Stowe charter which is dated AD956 which forms one of five Saxon charters which taken together show the fragmentation of a large royal estate (Brown *et al* 1981, 138).

When writing about Higham Ferrers, Hardy *et al* noted (2007, 199) that the area of the East Midlands is arguably the most obscure and poorly understood area of Lowland England at this time, principally because of a dearth of any detailed historical framework. For most sites around Wollaston the earliest written evidence surviving is the Domesday Book (1086). This fact is relevant as the Pioneer burial dated to some 400 years prior to this survey so trying to understand this burial in relation to the surrounding landscape using such documents needs many caveats. Wollaston is listed in the Domesday Book as having two manors one based on land of four thegns and the other owned by Stric (Hall 1977, 47-49). Foard using documentary records also pointed out (1985, fig 2 and appendix IV) that one hide within Wollaston in the Domesday Book had been within the estate centre of Yardley Hastings.

Since the discovery of the Pioneer burial Brown and Foard have suggested (2004, 91), "its location on the southern boundary of the Hundred of Higham Ferrers would indicate a person associated with the soke belonging to Higham Ferrers and Irthlingborough or possibly the princely house of the *provincia* of Oundle. A burial in this position was making a statement about territoriality." The suggestion of Brown and Foard is entirely possible but it should be noted that there is no surviving documentary evidence to support either suggestion. The only specific documentary reference to a unit of organisation above the soke which can be definitely related to Northamptonshire is the '*provincia* of Oundle' which is Bede's word for kingdom/sub-kingdom (Foard 1985, 193). Bede refers

Chapter 5 Discussion

to royal estate of Oundle under the government of the Abbot Cuthwold in AD709, but the actual boundaries are unknown (*Ibid*, 193).

Wollaston was near the south-eastern edge of what is called Outer Mercia, an area of secondary territories absorbed by Central Mercia in the 6th or early to middle 7th centuries. The Pioneer burial, was probably within the area of Middle Angles, a collective term for a number of groups or tribes which comprised small, possibly independent territories, whose name we know, but whose geographic extent is a matter of conjecture (Hunt 2016, 199; Foard 1985, 193; Courtney 1981, 91). In placing the burial within the context of the Mercian Kingdom which controlled the Wollaston area, it should be noted that it has been suggested that the Mercian kings of the 7th and 8th centuries never developed their concept of kingdoms beyond that of earlier times, and that Mercia never really evolved beyond a confederacy of sub-kingdoms (Hardy *et al* 2007, 201). It is also worth pointing out that it was the practice from the 7th century of setting up sub-kings or ealdorman to rule over the newly annexed Mercian provinces (Yorke 1990, 126). Foard (1999, 13-14) suggested that under the new sub-king, Peada, the Middle Angles were converted to Christianity and presumably as a result of this independent territories became provinces of Mercia and their central places were converted to provincial administrative centres. It is worth noting that in Middle Anglia the Tribal Hidage possibly written *c*AD670-690 (Davies and Verck 1974, 223-227) or in the late 8th century (Hart 1977) listed the tribes in the area by number of hides (Courtney 1981, 93-98). Foard suggested (1985, 200) that the surviving Tribal Hidage may have been a composite document dating to both periods. Bede describes one of these tribes, the ruler of the South Gyrwe (probably in the Peterborough area) as being 600 hides in size in around the mid-7th century as a *princeps* (Sherley-Price 1968, chapter 20; Courtney 1981, 93). This term is sometimes translated as 'ealdorman' but 'prince' would probably be more appropriate (*ibid*). The tribe which controlled the Wollaston area is uncertain, but the Pioneer burial may be seen in this light as the ruler of a tribe in the Middle Angle area or a member of its family for this location and the burial may have been located at the estate boundary. Grinsell thought (1991, 51) it is, "just possible that the Saxon may occasionally have built cairns or mounds to mark the bounds of their estates, especially where a suitable landmark was not already to hand."

The Pioneer burial was located near to the contemporary settlement of Wollaston but what status this settlement had in this period is uncertain due to the lack of surviving Saxon documentary evidence. David Hall nearly two decades before the Pioneer burial had been uncovered (1977) thought Wollaston had been a 'primary settlement' in the early to middle Saxon period and he grouped together Wollaston with the later parishes of Strixton, Bozeat and Easton Maudit as a single entity (*ibid*, fig 1 and 14-17). He noted that coin evidence, road pattern, and the later parish boundaries of this suggested to him that Wollaston was the chief settlement of this group. Hall grouped the four collectively, observing 'smooth' boundaries following brooks and watersheds. The coin evidence consisted of two Saxon coins found at Wollaston including a Mercian 'porcupine' sceates, a Type B which dated to the early 8th century (Metcalf 1977, including fig 8). In the early 8th century sceatta coin finds are concentrated in the eastern and southern frontier zones of the Mercian empire including Wollaston and this was primarily a consequence of interregional trade and not of military expenditure (*ibid*, 99-102). Hall noted that primary settlements, "would be expected to have roads leading fairly directly to all the neighbouring villages, with no road necessary leading fairly directly *through* the primary settlement in question. Later settlements will have been built on existing roads, and have additional roads to nearby places....it seems that all roads lead to Wollaston and none go through it" (Hall 1977, 17). The Higham Ferrers estate centre also lay at the junctions of important routes to the north and south along the River Nene, and to the south-east (Hardy *et al* 2007, 194).

Middle Saxon settlement and/or pottery evidence have been found on the western side of Wollaston in four locations (Hall 1977, fig 1; See Chapter 1). Subsequently a further excavation was undertaken at Dando Close where early to middle Saxon structures have been excavated (Semmelmann and Ashworth 2004). Just over a 1,000 pottery sherds were recovered from this excavation mostly dating from the 6th century and continuing into the middle Saxon period with 45 sherds of Maxey ware and three of Ipswich ware. Overall this may suggest that Wollaston had been a relatively large nucleated middle Saxon settlement. It is worth asking whether the presumed early Saxon occupation (a single SFB was found within a relatively small excavation), 1.5km to the east of the Pioneer burial, which was abandoned in the early 7th century (Chapman and Jackson 1992) moved to this nucleated location. It is interesting to note that some studies have concluded that when an early/ middle Saxon farmstead was abandoned, its inhabitants seem to have moved to a single larger and perhaps higher status settlement within the same territory (Jones and Page 2006, 81).

The date of settlement nucleation varies but major estate centres such as Higham Ferrers had presumably coalesced and certainly experienced deliberate development before AD 850 (Hardy *et al* 2007). In contrast, in lesser settlements within the Whittlewood part of Northamptonshire, the date tended to be after AD 850 (Jones and Page 2006, 103). At Cottenham, Cambridgeshire the indications are that the village became nucleated at or before the arrival of middle Saxon Ipswich ware pottery on the site (Mortimer 2000, 21). This move was part of the middle Saxon 'shuffle' - what is known as *schwerpunktverlagerung*.

In the late Saxon period Wollaston was still an important settlement within the Higham Ferrers Hundred. Hall suggests that the Hundred court may have originally been held in the area known as *Spytchehokes* in 1430 located at the northern edge of the Wollaston parish (Hall 1977, 20 and 26). The Domesday Book (1086) recorded 43 people in Wollaston including a priest which collectively was the highest number of people from a settlement recorded in the Hundred (*ibid*, 41 and 43).

Nature of the grave

Barrow mound

Examination by hand of the area around the grave failed to produce any signs of a quarry ditch but it is still likely that this burial lay beneath a barrow mound. The distance away from the road edge would allow the accommodation of a mound with a radius of up to 8m, a diameter of 16m, without interfering with the road.

No physical evidence for a mound was found during the excavation. This lack of evidence is not surprising considering the long history of this area being ploughed since at least the medieval period. The Pioneer burial was located in what would become Wollaston's medieval open field called Nether Field and presumably any mound was removed by arable farming over hundreds of years. Northamptonshire as a county was notably affected by arable farming and ridge and furrow has extensively been recorded including by Hall (1995).

The large size of the Pioneer grave, the evidence it had been an isolated burial placed overlooking the River Nene, probably at a significant land boundary and road junctions all point to the likelihood that it had been positioned here to be noticed. This might further suggest it had originally been beneath a mound. It is worth noting that the late 7th century has produced a series of isolated barrow-burials some of which were especially wealthy (Geake 1997). A barrow at Wollaston is probable but it should also be noted that an isolated rich burial excavated at Newark also produced no evidence for a barrow (Samuels and Russell 1999). Wills (2014, 2-3) points out the cut of the Pioneer burial, the age of the person buried and the grave goods within it are similar to Sutton Hoo Mound 17.

Burial within barrows, whether into prehistoric monuments or freshly constructed mounds is a well-known tradition of the Saxon period (Bateman 1848; 1861). The importance of this type of burial is highlighted by the fact that the context of known 'princely' burials is a regional research theme in the framework for the East Midlands (Vince 2006, 170 and 184). The closest surviving comparison to Wollaston is the isolated 'princely' burial under a mound at Taplow Court, Buckinghamshire which dated to the early 7th century and was a male weapon-burial with feasting gear (Webster 1992). We possibly even know the name of the individual buried as Taplow is translated as 'Taeppa's mound' (Farley 2010, 122). The location had similarities to the Pioneer burial being situated close to a chalk cliff overlooking the River Thames. Taeppa, assuming that was his name, was buried in a central grave 20 foot from the summit of the mound and six foot below the original ground level. He was fully dressed with gold threads from his jacket surviving and accompanied by a range of artefacts including a copper alloy hanging bowl. Other significant isolated barrows include one within the Roman enclosure on Lowbury Hill in Berkshire which was excavated in 1913. Geake (1999a, 8) records that it contained a skeleton on the same rough orientation as Wollaston with its head to the south, a hanging bowl, a sword, a shield, a spearhead, a knife, part of a pair of shears, a possible fire steel, a small bronze and a small iron buckle, a hump-backed antler comb in a wood and leather case and a rectangular strip of bone pierced at both ends.

Within the East Midlands region, barrow burials are best known from the Derbyshire Peak district. The Peak burials have been studied by several scholars (notably Ozanne 1962–3) and most recently re-evaluated by Howard Jones (1997). Previously, it has been claimed that the Peak burials are mainly 7th century, reflecting a late Saxon colonisation of this area, or even the imposition of Saxon overlords on a British population. Jones, however, finds evidence that the burials span a wider period and that in some cases the barrow burial may be associated with a larger, flat cemetery. The Peak burials include one 'princely' burial, at Benty Grange which is very similar to the Pioneer burial (Ozanne1962–3, 20–22). Six barrow burials are known from Lincolnshire, all containing accompanied inhumations. None of the six have been excavated under modern conditions. They include one 'princely' burial, at Caenby Corner; its context is unknown and clearly in need of investigation (Everson1993, 94–98).

In Northamptonshire Saxon barrows were probably not uncommon. There are up to eight other candidates for sites having Saxon barrows, but none had seemingly contained a princely burial. Of these eight possible mounds only one has been excavated by archaeological methods in recent times at Pineham Zone H, Northampton (Simmonds 2017). This work found an early Saxon ring ditch which had probably been a ploughed out barrow and had an external diameter of 15.2m. It was located at 73m aOD with the River Nene less than 1km to the north and a stream *c*300m to the south but no burials were found within it. The ring ditch cut a late Bronze Age pit alignment and the primary fill of the Pineham ring ditch itself has been radiocarbon dated to 590-665 cal AD, 1410 ± 30 BP, at 95% certainty; Beta-497183. An inhumation cemetery of seven burials respected the Pineham ring ditch on both its northern and southern sides. One of the burials contained a Swanton Type C3 spear head which has been provisionally been dated from the 6th century to 7th century AD.

The Northamptonshire HER records four other possible Saxon barrows, but none of these were recorded in the recent era. At Thenford, South Northants at least seven skeletons with grave goods (knife and vessels) were found in a large mound prior to AD1830 (NHER 184/1/1). A possible early Saxon barrow was found at Norton, near Daventry (NHER 888/0/1). It had a low mound 40-50m long, 2/3m wide and 1m high which was levelled 1855/6 but was recorded in 1868 as containing five to six inhumations with grave goods comprising a knife, brooches, rings, beads, spindle whorl and sleeve clasp. The records (1933) are poor for a possible Saxon barrow in Northampton. It is uncertain whether this barrow had contained an inhumation buried with a knife, or whether this barrow / ring ditch had been adjacent to the burial (NHER 1695/0/1). Another barrow in Northampton has been postulated at Cow Meadow it was destroyed in 19th century and contained cinerary urns, brooch, pin, buckle and tweezers (NHER 5210/0/1). In addition O'Brien (1999, 102-3) lists a further three sites comprising a small barrow on the top of the inner vallum at the Iron Age hillfort at Borough Hill, Daventry, a female burial at Abington, Northampton and a cremation from Pitsford, near Daventry.

The grave

The size of the Pioneer grave was far greater than that generally necessary for a single inhumation. The great size, whilst possibly a reflection of the enthusiasm of the gravediggers, could reflect a purpose; it was presumably dug with the explicit intension of creating a sizeable area to receive both the inhumed body and the range of artefacts. It is possible to suggest, from several individually inconclusive pieces of evidence that this body had been laid on a bed that required the large grave. At Wollaston parts of the grave had notable amount of 'space' where there were no surviving archaeological remains (including artefacts; See Chapter 2). It is uncertain whether this was deliberate, accidental or if there had previously been artefacts which did not survive in the archaeological record either due to truncation and/or that they were perishable. The Wollaston over size grave has similarities with other sites including at Snape, Norfolk where many of the graves were considerably larger than was necessary to contain a body (Filmer-Sankey and Pestell 2001).

During the initial examination of the body and artefacts in the grave, it was noted that the remains were some distance above the base of the cut. The position of the skull and hanging bowl may suggest the presence a pillow. The skull and mandible had slipped sideways from each other, suggesting the movement had occurred slowly but not in a void such as a coffin. Such movement might be expected if the head had been placed on a pillow or cushion which, as it decayed, slowly allowed the disarticulating bones to displace. The hanging bowl lay on edge behind the skull as if it had rolled off a surface such as a pillow. The position of the fragments of leg bone was also such that a normally articulated body with the head resting on a pillow, could not attain without some degree of post depositional settlement. Pillows have been identified with burials at Valsgarde 6, Oseberg and Morken (Bruce-Mitford 1974, 415).

During the initial examination of the surface of the helmet minerally preserved organic remains were observed. These appeared to represent feathers but the sampled examples were later seen to be roots (See Read, Chapter 3) and textiles, the latter most probably associated with bedding rather than clothing. Although no iron bed fittings like those recovered from Swallowcliffe (Speake 1989) or Barrington (Malim and Hines 1998) were present, this would not preclude the existence of a bed in the grave. At a basic level it could have comprised a mattress and pillow but it is possible that a wooden frame may have been present. A bed frame constructed entirely of wood occurred in the grave of a prince under Cologne Cathedral (Speake 1989, 114); a variant of this would have left no trace in the light gravel soils of Wollaston.

Within the grave and beyond the bowl lay a single large irregular bunter pebble. Although these are infrequently present in the gravel they do not occur in the ploughsoil. This example must have been carefully selected for burial in the grave, its size would not allow for its accidental incorporation in the grave fill. The purpose of a single stone in a grave is difficult to understand, multiple stones are often arranged around a grave cut to form a discontinuous lining but single stones suggest a much more deliberate and considered inclusion. It is possible it served a quite prosaic role in supporting the bed or the head but a more likely reason for its presence is that it was part of some unrecognised funerary requirement. Several graves containing single stones close to the head were present in the Great Chesterford, Essex cemetery, graves 9, 53, 124 and the horse burial 142 (Evison 1994), unfortunately the report does not specify the type of stone. At Snape, Norfolk there was a large quartzite stone in grave 47 (Filmer-Sankey and Pestell 2001, fig 4.4).

The sword lay diagonally across the lower body, the grip where the left hip would have been with the blade pointing to below the right knee. The iron knife was located about 20mm from the grip and in a parallel axis, perhaps indicating that it had been inserted into the upper part of the sword scabbard. Generally knives in graves where associated with swords are in positions that indicate they were separately sheathed for example Westgarth, Suffolk, graves 51 and 66 (West 1988) and Alton, Hampshire, graves 1, 16 and 42 (Evison 1988).

Importance of the burial

The Pioneer burial is dated to the later 7th century on the basis of the style of belt buckles found in the grave and this suggests a *terminus post quem* for the burial (See Meadows, Chapter 3 citing Hirst 1985, 86; Marzinzik 2003, type group 11.24b). Such a date ties in with analysis of burials through grave goods and radiocarbon dating which suggests that furnished burials cease in the late 7th century rather than in the early decades of the 8th century as some had previously believed (Bayliss et al 2013, 554). Geake notes that the 7th and early 8th-century homogeneity in burial artefacts has been recognised for some time and she saw there was a strong classical influence in grave goods of this period (Geake 1999b, 205 and 209).

Research (Hunt 2016, 129) has shown that the archaeology of early Saxon inhumation burials suggests a society familiar with hierarchy and a sense of 'one's place' within the community. The variability of grave goods has been regarded as an index of social position and wealth (e.g. Alcock 1981; Hunt 2016, 129). Artefacts were probably selected from a number of sources including possessions of the dead, their kin, and possibly participants at the funeral. The Pioneer burial should be seen in relation to the fact that early Saxon cemeteries in Mercia contain well-equipped warrior burials suggestive of a male elite and richly furnished females reflecting the apparent prominence of powerful women (Hunt 2016, 129). The words 'warrior burial' also includes probable teenagers such as an example at Castledyke South, Barton-on-Humber, where grave 179, probably dating to the 7th century, contained an inhumation aged 12 to 16 with grave goods comprising a sword, hanging bowl and a spear (Drinkall and Foreman 1998, 314-331).

The Wollaston grave goods suggest that the individual was of a social standing above that of the ordinary Saxon warrior burials by including a helmet, a cooper alloy hanging bowl and a high quality pattern welded sword. We have seen that the burial was in the late Saxon parish of Wollaston in which there was a probable primary settlement at a key location (see above). The other Pioneer burial goods (three buckles, a clothing hook and a knife) do not mark the burial as 'special', but would be seen of functionally important in the afterlife. For this reason buckles and the knives are near-ubiquitous items in Saxon graves of all periods, in contrast with the rarity of helmets, hanging bowls and pattern-welded swords (Lucy 2000, 58).

Through the 7th century on some sites the type of grave goods including weapons contained in burials were increasing displayed by the grave being left open allowing the witnessing of the burial as a sign of status (Härke 1992). Härke commented (1990, 26) that helmets and mail corselets were the least common weapon-types, found only in a few of the richest graves. Härke interpreted (1990; 1992) the presence of weapons (and the choice of weapon combinations) as forming a multi-layered set of meanings including symbolic act relating to the social identity of the deceased. Härke also suggested (1997) that the burial of weapons had an ethnically Germanic origin, symbolising perceived and/or real cultural origins through the burial ritual. The helmet at Wollaston with the boar-crest certainly evokes the scenes described in the Beowulf poem.

The high quality weapons in the Pioneer burial partly mattered as Saxon armies were relatively small and any advantage over opponents was especially important. Davies quotes (2004, 23) Hawkes suggestion that a Saxon army typically numbered 80-200 and Hines estimation was of 250 men. Caple (forthcoming) therefore says that with armies this small, most conflicts involved just a few tens of men and the action of the individual warrior mattered. He noted that, "the high quality steeled weapons recovered from the graves of kings and warriors may have provided a significant advantage in individual combat situations, their decorated form emphasising their symbolic power and prestige of their owner." In contrast battles from the 11th century comprised thousands of people, for example the Norman forces at Hastings are estimated at between 6000 and 7500 (Morillo 1994; Gravett 1992), and here the activities of an individual soldier rarely mattered.

Helmet

The most significant grave good from the Pioneer burial was the helmet. They are extremely rare and only found, so far, in four or possibly five grave contexts in England over the last 150 or so years and a few helmets or parts of have been found from non-burial contexts (Figs 5.2 and 5.4).

Helmet burials were found across the eastern, midland and southern Britain. Up to four examples, including the Pioneer helmet are of Nordic-influenced crested type. The other examples of this helmet type, one from the royal cemetery at Sutton Hoo, Suffolk, found in 1939 (Carver 1998), another was found at Benty Grange, Derbyshire (Bateman 1861) and a third was possibly at Guilden Morden, Cambridgeshire in *c*1864 (Fordham 1904). A further helmet dating to the early Saxon period, of the continental Frankish style, has been found in a burial at Shorwell, Isle of Wight in 2004 (Hood et al 2012). The occurrence of only three definite other middle Saxon helmets within graves, despite

CHAPTER 5 DISCUSSION

FIGURE 5.4. ARTIST'S IMPRESSION OF THE PIONEER HELMET

thousands of graves of this period being excavated in England, illustrates the rarity of such pieces. It is unclear whether the rarity is a reflection of the value of such pieces or true scarceness. It is possible there had been other helmets deposited in graves but Geake suggests (1999b, 204) that they were possibly under-represented in the archaeological record due to poor survival. It is possible some helmets may have been mistaken for other objects such as buckets, but any such numbers would have been few. Other possible reasons may be that in many cases the helm may have been of beaten leather or that helmets may have been passed down from father to son, for example the Coppergate helmet was old when deposited in a pit.

In addition to helmets from burials, at least two other helmets/parts of helmets are known from other contexts. At York an 8th century helmet was found in a domestic feature at Coppergate (Tweddle 1992) and parts of at least one helmet was recovered in the Staffordshire Hoard (Fern *et al* in prep). Presumably gold/silver elements from helmets got melted down, which was possibly the intended fate of those fragments recovered from the Staffordshire Hoard. Helmets are also scarce throughout north-west Europe in the 6th to 8th century (Caple forthcoming).

As well as these early and middle Saxon helmets, a 10th century Viking helmet has been uncovered in the 1950s at Yarm, Yorkshire but the archaeological context is uncertain. It was found by workmen during the laying of sewer pipes, and had possibly originally been hidden or discarded in a pit. The Yarm helmet has some similarities with the earlier helmets being somewhat between the hemispherical domed shape of the Pioneer helmet and the later conical form of the nasal helmets (Caple forthcoming). The only direct parallels for the Yarm helmet are from the continent.

Overall the scarcity of helmets in the archaeological record for the Saxon period is probably a fair reflection as they were perhaps not seen as a normal burial good. This was presumably due to such reasons as the cost of construction and the need for a very skilled craftsman – such objects were not given away lightly even to accompany the burial of an important person.

Even though helmets were not a typical grave good, all four burials definitely containing one had similarities implying that some classes of grave goods were associated with each other. The most obvious is that all four burials also contained at least one copper alloy hanging bowl. However, it is also worth recording the differences between the burials as these were many. A comparison of all burials (as well as the possible Guilden Morden, Cambridgeshire example) is given below:

1) Sutton Hoo, mound 1 was a ship burial within a small very high status burial ground. It had a chamber lined with fabrics and hangings and many artefacts. These included a coffin, a pillow, shoes, an impressive parade helmet (designed for show and visual impact and seems to have been on top of the coffin), three hanging bowls, spears, sword, bottles, horns, lyre, bucket, mailcoat, flowers, toilet bowl, cap, ladle, wooden bottles, combs, gaming pieces, a bell, spoons, silver dish, shield, iron 'standard' and an iron lamp. The date of Mound 1 depends on when the associated coins were assembled; this is usually quoted as after *c*AD620-25 (Geeke 1999a, 8).

2) Benty Grange was an isolated barrow burial dated to the 2nd half of the 7th century on stylistic grounds of the boar-crested helmet recovered (Bruce-Mitford 1974, 242). The burial may have had a planked chamber (O'Brien 1999, 91). Other artefacts within the grave included the probable hanging bowl (three hanging bowl discs were found), a pile cloak, some chain perhaps from a cauldron, some silver mounts from a cup, and an iron implement 'very much like an ordinary hayfork'.

3) The Shorwell helmet was found in a burial ground, it dates to a far earlier period *c*AD500-550. There was no evidence for a mound over

this grave which was 'normal size' *c*2m long by 0.5m wide. It is worth pointing out apart from the grave goods with this burial there were no other distinguishing characteristics to mark is out from all the other graves in the cemetery. The grave had not even been dug to a great depth and as a result it had been severely disturbed by ploughing. In the grave were other objects such as a pattern-welded sword, a hanging bowl, shield boss, copper alloy buckle, fluted glass vessel fragments and a gold coin recovered nearby which dated to AD491–518 may also be associated with the burial. The helmet was similar to the Pioneer helmet in being made of iron, exhibiting hardly any decoration other than a speculative exterior leather covering, and was a utilitarian fighting helmet (Hood *et al* 2012). This report speculated it had been a high status male 'warrior' burial possibly that of a Frank serving in the retinue of the local ruler.

4) A copper alloy boar figurine was recovered at Guilden Morden, Cambridgeshire in 1864 or 1865 during coprolite digging (Fordham 1904, 373-4). The son of the person who found the figurine in his recollections 40 years after the discovery stated he thought it had been recovered from the subsoil, at no great depth, probably in a grave. He thought the boar, an earthenware bead and various other objects (all subsequently lost) had originally hung round the neck of the person buried. This description led Foster to state (1977, 166) that, "there is some evidence that the Guilden Morden boar formed part of a pagan Saxon grave group". Both Fordham and Foster suggest that the Guilden Morden boar may have originally been attached to the crest of a helmet (Fordham 1904, 374; Foster 1977, 167).

The helmet material in the Staffordshire Hoard was recovered in over 1000 fragments, most of which were from decorated silver sheet, bearing designs of warriors and Style II animal art similar to the helmets from Sutton Hoo and the Swedish sites of Vendel and Valsgärde (Fern *et al* in prep). The only structural parts that survive in the Staffordshire Hoard are a cast silver-gilt crest and pair of silver-gilt cheek-pieces that are *en suite*, also with Style II animal ornament, as well as remains of a silver band that ran around the circumference (*pers comm*, Chris Fern). There were no remains of the iron or leatherwork of the helmet (or helmets), from which the precious metal-parts were stripped. The helmet in the Staffordshire Hoard was therefore of similar quality to the Sutton Hoo helmet and contrasted with the Pioneer helmet. It also did not have a boar-crest like the Pioneer helmet or Benty Grange example, and no other such crests were contained in the hoard.

The Pioneer and Sutton Hoo burials were deliberately placed overlooking prominent rivers whilst the Benty Grange and the Pioneer burial were located adjacent to Roman routeways. The Benty Grange burial was at a high location on bleak situation in the Peak District (Bateman 1861, 28). The location of the Guilden Morden possible burial is uncertain.

Of the helmets in burials the Shorwell and Pioneer examples look to be true helmets meant to be worn in battle – it is uncertain whether the others could be also described as this. The Pioneer and Shorwell helmets are plain (in case of the Pioneer helmet the exception is the boar crest and the shallow incised line; this again may reflect the functionality of the piece). The Pioneer helmet is therefore a utilitarian piece with little decoration; it originally consisted of an iron skull cap, from which hung two cheek guards. The form of neck protection that the helmet afforded, if any, is uncertain, owing to ploughing damage to that part of the helmet. Saxon literature is full of heroes engaged in battles but neither the Benty Grange nor the Sutton Hoo ones would have been practical in such a situation. Even the York, Coppergate helmet, with its chain mail aventail, would have afforded little protection in a conflict owing to the small size of its cap. In contrast the Wollaston helmet is large, its internal area is such that to wear it a substantial body of lining and padding is required which both raises the crest high above the wearer and protects the head of the wearer from any impacts. The Viking helmet from Yarm was similarly a utilitarian helmet also composed of iron bands and plates (Caple forthcoming). Caple noted that care was taken to ensure the rivets on the Yarm helmet exterior were hammered flush to the surface and this was also seen on the Shorwell, Coppergate and Pioneer helmets. This was presumably to avoid catching bladed weapons which could come into contact with the helmet exterior, giving excellent deflective and thus defensive qualities.

The Pioneer helmet was the most sparsely decorated and most utilitarian of these helmets (apart from Shorwell and Yarm), but has some comparisons with the others. Its basic form is very similar to the Coppergate helmet from York but it is larger and lacks the copper alloy details. The Pioneer helmet's boar is smaller, simpler and made in iron whilst the Guilden Morden boar which was fashioned in copper alloy and has a large crest running down its back and the Benty Grange boar is studded with silver and has garnet and silver filigree eyes. The boar crest on the Pioneer, Benty Grange and Guilden Morden helmets is part of a tradition best known from literature such as Beowulf. Boar crests are almost commonplaces of heroes in this epic poem in which boar-adorned helmets are mentioned five times. The poem speaks also of a funeral pyre "heaped with boar-shaped helmets forged in gold (Heaney 2000, 77). Despite this there have only been two or three boar-crested helmets or parts of uncovered in England (the Pioneer and Benty Grange helmets and a single possible detached boar crest have been found at Guilden Morden, Cambridgeshire (this volume; Bateman 1861; Foster 1977).

The boar appears to have the symbolic value of strength as well as the possible religious association as a familiar with the Germanic goddess Freyja (Frank 2008). The importance seems to have started far earlier. For example the 1st century AD Roman historian Tacitus suggested that the Balti Aesti wore boar symbols in battle to invoke her protection (Church and Brodribb 1868).

In contrast with the other helmets from England the Pioneer example was 'ritually killed' by having its nasal guard bent back into the helmet. Not only are there no other English helmets treated in such a way but no continental examples of helmets from graves have undergone pre depositional damage. The rendering objects unfit for use serves to break their link with this world and is a well known practice but rich artefacts such as helmets elsewhere seem to have escaped it. It is unclear why this helmet was treated in this way.

Hanging bowl

Hanging bowls are extremely uncommon in graves before the 7th century with Shorwell, a 6th century example being an exception, but this burial was possibly a Frank (Hood *et al* 2012). Before the Shorwell example had been found it had been thought that the helmet and hanging bowls were two 'new' grave-good type used only from the 7th century. It had been recorded that although hanging bowls were exclusively found in graves dating to the 7th and 8th centuries, they had become 'popular' as grave gods in the second half of the 7th century (Geake 1999b, 204 and 209). Hanging bowls are rare, the admittedly somewhat dated statistic from the late 20th century, has recorded that they have only been found in around 50 graves of which 24 graves could be dated (Geake 1999a, 2-3). The Wollaston hanging bowl would fall into Geake's 1999a Group D: Hanging bowl graves which can be dated by their associated grave-goods. A few of the graves which contained a hanging bowl also had a sword or in one case a short sword (seax).

The presence of a hanging bowl, even an old and damaged one, was a significant marker. Less than 200 of these vessels exist (including from non-funerary contexts), a scarcity that itself suggests they are special objects. The Wollaston bowl with its repair and missing escutcheons has clearly been a prized heirloom prior to its final deposition in the grave. This view is reinforced by the fact that all three of the bowls from Sutton Hoo had been repaired in antiquity (Bruce-Mitford op cit, 290).

In Northamptonshire only parts of four other possible hanging bowls have been found. At Cransley, near Kettering (NHER 3680/1/1) part of a hanging bowl may have been recovered amongst other artefacts in a grave uncovered in the 19th century (see below; O'Brien 1999, 103). Part of a hanging bowl was reported to the Portable Antiquities Scheme (PAS) in 2000 (FNN108250; NARC- 728; Monument ID 7598/0/0). An escutcheon from a hanging bowl dated *c*AD550-700 was found in 2018 at Nether Heyford and reported to PAS (NARC-165018). At Duston, Northampton there was possibly part of a hanging bowl recorded (O'Brien 1999, 103).

Pattern-welded sword

The sword is again a rare but not unique object in rich graves of this period, this example is however of highly complex workmanship making it amongst the best pattern-welded swords of the period. It would appear that rods had been forged together in a pattern weld and there were on average 4-5 rods in each strip for the sword (See Meadows, Chapter 3). The sword and the bowl together would signify a rich burial but are not extraordinary finds from graves; the helmet however is an exceptional object. Swords of any type or quality were comparatively scarce even in weapon burials and were prestige goods and symbols of an aristocratic class (Bone 1989, 69). They were more common in earlier Saxon burials, declining as grave goods in the 7th century (Geake 1997, 1). Härke in his study of weapon burial rite noted that only 18% of his corpus of 3,814 inhumations from 47 cemeteries contained weapons (Härke 1990, 25). Up to one in ten of these weapon burials contained a sword, seax, axe or arrows. Härke estimated the weapon burial rite reached a peak in the mid-6th century and sharply declines after that, virtually going out of use by AD700 (*ibid*, 30).

There were probable early to middle Saxon sword burials at only four other sites in Northamptonshire (Badby, Cransley, Nether Heyford and Thorpe Malsor). Brown and Foard state (2004, 85) that, "Certain men were given weapons, swords being the most prestigious; very few burials from Northamptonshire had these, and the (19th century) records, which suggest sword burials at Badby, Cransley and Thorpe Malsor, are early and not very reliable". Northamptonshire has 58 pagan cemeteries recorded with both cremation and inhumation rites practiced (Brown and Foard 2004, 82). Given the relatively large number of known Saxon cemeteries in Northamptonshire the numbers of graves containing swords are few. This can be seen at Wakerley where none of the largely 6th century cemetery, which comprised 85 burials, contained swords (Adams and Jackson 1989).

The date of the burials containing swords in the county has only been dated accurately at Whitehall Farm, Nether Heyford (radiocarbon date) and the Pioneer burial (artefacts) and both these are seemingly of the middle to late 7th century 'Christian' conversion period. At Whitehall Farm two inhumations including one with a sword, were originally found by metal detectorists and subsequently archaeologically excavated (Upson-Smith 2000). The possible earlier burial of the two may have been a female and lay east to west and probably dated to the 5th century AD, being one of a number of burials dating to *c*AD420-480 (*pers comm*, Stephen Young). This was cut by the second grave with the body of a young man in a semi-crouched position also orientated east to west with head at the western side and his legs and upper body lying on the left side. The young man was accompanied with a sword on his right side and an iron knife (Upson-Smith 2000, 1-2 and fig 3; Brown and Foard 2004, 87; NHER 9192/1/1). A radiocarbon date for this burial produced a date from the middle 7th century (640-870 cal AD, 1306±51BP, 95.4% probability (WK-11234)). Probably significant was the main spike in the date range lay between AD660-730 (45.4% probability). X-rays show the Whitehall Farm sword is pattern-welded with a steel edge on one side making an effective weapon if not of the best quality (*pers comm*, Stephen Young). The arrangement and date of this burial led Brown and Foard to speculate (2004, 87) that we may be seeing here evidence for the transition to Christianity.

The other burials containing swords in Northamptonshire are from Badby, near Daventry (NHER 480/1/1), Cransley, near Kettering (NHER 3680/1/1) and Thorpe Malsor, Kettering (NHER 3681/1/1). The Badby example was found by workmen just over 1km south and east of Badby in the middle 19th century. Notes were taken from the workmen in April 1843 concerned the large number of skeletons they uncovered over the previous 12 years and amongst the artefacts they claimed to have found were some swords. Some artefacts survive (beads, rings, pins, brooches etc. but none of the knives or swords). At Cransley a number of finds made from 1879 onwards but were only first recorded first in 1902. At a depth of *c*1m human remains were discovered (male and female), but they did not record any other details. Artefacts recovered include part of a sword, a possible copper alloy (?hanging) bowl, a possible copper alloy drinking horn, a spearhead, brooches, a silver ring, a pottery jug, beads, and a blade. At Thorpe Malsor at least two burials were found in 1910 whilst ironstone mining. The artefacts recovered comprised a sword fragment, two spearheads, shield bosses, wrist clasps, two brooches and a pottery vessel. In addition to these swords an isolated burial at Clipston, near Daventry (NHER 6190/0/1) had grave goods consisting of a seax, spear and a knife.

Pioneer burial and 'Christianity'

The Pioneer burial is dated to the late 7th century by associated artefacts, particularly the narrow belt buckles. He was therefore buried at a significant time of religious change and changing burial customs. It is also at a time when relatively few burials of this date are known from Northamptonshire or the East Midlands in general. The late Alan Vince (2006, 166) noted that late 7th to 9th century cemeteries of any size have rarely been excavated in the East Midlands. Vince stated this period was a 'missing' phase between pagan cemeteries and the establishment of most parish churches in the 10th and 11th century.

Northamptonshire was within the area of the Mercian kingdom which controlled this area sometime before the middle of the 7th century. It is important to note the Mercian kingdom converted from paganism to Christianity under King Penda over AD653-655 (Sherley-Price 1968, 176-7). On Peada's death Diuma was appointed the first bishop of Mercia and Middle Anglia, but it should be noticed that Bede stated that a shortage of priests made it necessary for one bishop to serve both peoples (Sherley-Price 1968, chapters 21 and 24). Later, Wollaston presumably fell within the bishopric of Lichfield which was created in the late 7th century but later fell within the new bishopric of Leicester in AD737 (Hunt 2016, 45-7).

The lack of priests in the mid to late 7th century may suggest that Christianity would have taken some time to become dominant in these Middle Anglian and Mercian areas. The Pioneer burial, which may have been 'pagan' in nature, may be seen in this light, with the implication that some people in the Middle Anglian area even at the highest social positions (and presumably at least some of those who buried him) were still committed to the 'old' ways. Pendas two sons had encouraged in Mercia an effective diocesan structure and a network of minsters (*ibid*, 51). This may not however apply to all and indication of the religious leanings of the inhabitants of the Kingdom of Mercia, including Northamptonshire, in this period, are a subject which at best can be described as 'ambiguous' (Meaney 2003, 240-1). Other possible examples of both Christian and pagan affinities may have been found at Boss Hall, Ipswich. Here a woman of the Anglian élite was buried in an earlier pagan cemetery but the style of her burial suggests she was a Christian (Webster and Backhouse 1991, 52-3). The Benty Grange helmet has both a silver cross on the nose-piece as well as its 'protective' boar crest. The Sutton Hoo burial complex has produced evidence of 'Christian' and pagan associations and the Christian element can be seen in spoons recovered bearing the complementary names, Saul and Paul, which may been a baptismal present for a convert (Bruce-Mitford 1972, 68).

The Pioneer burial may fall within the typology of middle Saxon cemeteries with furnished graves often referred to as 'Final Phase' cemeteries (i.e. the final phase of furnished burial) within the conversion period. Whilst traditional scholarship has focused on the use of such sites to map religious conversion, more recently, burials of this period have been associated with changes to 'mentality and ideology' rather than more strictly with a change to religion or society (Geake 2003). While it has been proposed that this sort of Final Phase burial ground somehow maps religious conversion by representing the transition between a pagan furnished burial tradition of the 5th-6th centuries and the later Christian formalised cemetery, it has been determined that the church itself probably had little influence over burial rites in this period (Geake 2003; Hadley 2001). Williams states that grave goods and their usage in Final Phase burials should be understood as more than merely "'pagan survivals' or as manifestations of 'popular superstitions' but as the results of conscious and strategic mortuary decisions by the living about the identities of the dead" (Williams 2010, 27, 27). If this is the case then the Pioneer burial and/or and the people burying him were deliberately flouting the 'Christian' way presumably against the wishes of the king and the church.

The Wollaston burial was high status and the burial ritual may have been a significant occasion. As such it is worth considering Williams's comments (2006, 61), quoting other specialists, that when considering weapons we must be aware that the community and those controlling the burial ritual (elders, shamans or cunning women) as well as those looking on (relatives, allies, friends, subordinate groups, hired mourners etc.), may have had a clear set of expectations formed by social memory concerning how the dead should be disposed of. Graves may have been a method of social display, and as a vehicle for renegotiating and expressing concepts of 'personhood' and identity (Williams 2010, 27).

Artefacts may be present because of their meanings in terms of symbolism (Williams 2006, 38). The curated hanging bowl may have been chosen, for example, to evoke the past. The Pioneer burial may be seen in the context that even contemporary 'Christian' burials of this mid to late 7th century period were often buried with grave goods and personal possessions as these older rites must have been difficult to abandon.

Explanations other than religion have therefore been sought for this shifting pattern of grave goods and burial practice (Williams 2010, 27). Possible aspects affecting burial rite in this period may include socio-economic pressures brought about by political changes, increase in social stratification, alterations to law, inheritance, land use and ownership; as well as societal shift in the understanding of gender, status, age and ethnicity, and the use of symbols and mortuary practice to present and mediate these identities (Williams 2010, 27; Härke 1992, 149).

The Whitehall Farm sword burial, Nether Heyford (see above) was also radiocarbon dated to the same middle Saxon 'Christian' period as the Pioneer burial and may be seen in the same light of whether its burial rituals were pagan and/or Christian. This sword burial may have been the latest burial in a well-used old burial area and the only one yet found dating to this middle Saxon period – in this respect it is also similar to the Pioneer burial in being an 'isolated' interment. The difference between them was the sword burial was located within an area where there were at least 16 other burials of two different earlier periods and these have largely been excavated by Community Landscape Archaeological Survey Project (CLASP). The earliest burials are a group radiocarbon dated to between AD420 - 480 which is matched by the dates ascribed to their grave goods (*pers comm*, Stephen Young). These burials says Young correspond nicely with the timber phase hall construction over the site of the Roman villa by the mid the 5th century AD which was destroyed by fire by the mid-6th century AD. The second phase of burials are a small group of distinctive graves which lie immediately to the south of the 5th century burials and comprised 'pagan' burials which dated to the 6th to early 7th century.

Contemporary probable Christian burial comparisons

The Pioneer burial was aligned approximately south-east-south to north-west-north with his head to the south-eastern side and placed to look towards the River Nene to the north-west. The burial was therefore not aligned east to west as most 'Christian' burials were of this period although not all Final Phased burials were and this difference of alignment may not discount the Pioneer burial from being a Christian. A nearby example of different alignment of burials in the Christian reconversion period is Site H, A5M1 (Bedfordshire), also in the Mercian territory, where nine inhumation burials dating from the mid–late 7th century were scattered over an area of *c*40m by 25m. Seven of these burials were aligned north-west to south-east and four of these had the heads at the north-west end, one was aligned north–south with the head to the south, and one was aligned east–west with the head to the west (Brown forthcoming). Another example of diversity of orientation was at Chamberlain's Barn, Leighton Buzzard, Bedfordshire where a large Final Phase cemetery a minority of burials were not aligned east to west including 18 scattered burials with a high degree of variation in grave direction (Hyslop 1963, figs 2 and 3).

Other possible Northamptonshire burials contemporary with the Pioneer burial include a site at The Coach House, Middleton Cheney, Northamptonshire (NHER 5832/0/1). Three people (a man, women and child) were buried in a single grave orientated east to west with their heads at the western end. No other graves were found in the area in the subsequent watching brief with just two intercutting ditches in this general location containing 11th to 12th century pottery (Muldowney 2013). The Northamptonshire HER records that one of the burials produced a radiocarbon date between AD652 to 890 and calls them 'possible Christian burials'. The HER noted whilst the alignment of the burials was consistent for

Christianity rituals, the alignment may equally have been dictated by the east to west orientation of the property boundaries in the area.

Other contemporary burials in Northamptonshire are not Final Phase, but either from open-ground cemeteries or from churches themselves. A nearby example was at Great Houghton, Northampton where the open-ground middle Saxon cemetery was dated to about the 2nd half of the 7th century. It comprised 17 adults to six sub-adults, all without grave goods, within a c15m by 10m area in east to west rows (Chapman 2001). One of the burials (sk222) was radiocarbon dated to 635–785 cal AD, 1340± 50 BP, 95% probability (Beta-116572).

It should also be noted that churches in this region were being established in this same time period. The Anglo-Saxon Chronicle, for example, recorded that the monastery at Peterborough was started in AD654 by Penda's son Peada who also brought four priests to convert the people (manuscript E, 654-6; Swanton 1996; Sherley-Price 1968, Chapter 21). Other probable nearby churches are not as closely documented, but their origins may have been broadly contemporary with the Pioneer burial. St Peters, Northampton was probably established in the late 7th to mid-8th century (*pers comm*, Andy Chapman). At St Gregory's Northampton, an early ecclesiastical site is suggested by radiocarbon dates obtained from three east to west aligned burials in its graveyard, which produced middle to late Saxon dates (Brown and Foard 2004, 94; NHER 1160/5/1; Chapman forthcoming). Radiocarbon dates from these three burials (C315, C410 and C408) were recorded as dating respectively between the following dates: 580-890 cal AD, 1360 ± 100, 91% confidence (Har-4390); 650-900 cal AD, 1260 ± 70 BP, 93% confidence (Har-4810); 765-1020 cal AD, 1140± 70 BP, 91% confidence (Har-4809).

A small part of another contemporary cemetery has been excavated at Harringworth, Northamptonshire which was probably part a former minster church burial ground (Atkins 2004). Here radiocarbon dates placed the cemetery to the middle to late Saxon period. All burials were in east to west rows and none contained grave goods. Based on radiocarbon dates the upper burials at Harringworth were probably reusing plots perhaps more than a generation later, with the lower burials likely to date from around the mid 7th into 8th centuries while the later burials were 8th to mid-9th century.

At the probable middle to late Saxon minster burial ground area at Rothley, Leicestershire the interments included burial 153 which was found in a probable advance level of decay suggesting it had been transported some distance for burial (Upson-Smith 2016, 132). This led the author to suggest that burials were being received from outlying settlements to the mother/minster church (*ibid*, 132). The Pioneer burial was similar in that there may have been some time before the person was buried, but instead of taking him to a Christian minster church or an open-ground cemetery he was seemingly buried in a pagan way next to the River Nene.

Conclusions

The 'princely' Pioneer burial is an archaeological find of great importance; a rare discovery, it gives us a glimpse of how the hierarchical society of the middle to late 7th century used mortuary practice as a mechanism to influence and be a permanent reminder to the populace.

The type of grave goods accompanying this individual marks the burial as special, being one of only a handful in the country where a middle Saxon helmet has been recovered and together with the pattern-welded sword and hanging bowl strongly suggests this had been a high status individual. The isolated nature of this burial and its location is also significant particularly as he was buried during or after the reconversion to Christianity of the Mercian area. Remembrance seems to be key to this internment event – this elite individual had been buried next to a river, adjacent to a Roman road and at a possible important land division. Circumstantial archaeological evidence also suggests that he had been buried under a mound. Whether he had been pagan and/or Christian is uncertain, but the method of burial had more similarities with pagan practices.

This Pioneer burial therefore can be seen as very similar to other 'princely' burials including Benty Grange. It also had the same attributes, but not the same wealth or status, as the 'kingly' cemetery at Sutton Hoo. Elites can therefore be seen to be buried to be noticed in a different way to the contemporary general populace who were largely either buried mostly unadorned in minster churches or within small or medium sized cemeteries in open areas where they were either unadorned or had lesser grave goods compared to the 'princely' burials.

Bibliography

Adams, B, and Jackson, D, 1989 The Anglo-Saxon cemetery at Wakerley, Northamptonshire, Excavations by Mr D Jackson 1968-9, *Northamptonshire Archaeology,* **22**, 69-183

Alcock, L, 1981 Quantity or quality: the Anglian graves of Bernicia, in V Evison (ed), *Angles, Saxons and Jutes*, Oxford, 168-186

Arnold, C J, 1982 *The Anglo-Saxon cemeteries of the Isle of White*, British Museum Press

Atkins, R, 2004 A middle to late Saxon cemetery at Seaton Road, Harringworth, *Northamptonshire Archaeology,* **32**, 95-106

Atkins, R, 2018 *Late Iron Age and Roman settlement at Bozeat Quarry, Northamptonshire: excavations 1995-2016*, Archaeopress

Bateman, T, 1848 *Vestiges of the antiquities of Derbyshire*, London and Derby

Bateman, T, 1861 *Ten years diggings in Celtic and Saxon Grave Hills in the Counties of Derby, Stafford and York from 1848 to 1858,* 28-33, London

Bayley, J, 2000 Workshop technology; non-ferrous metallurgy, in A Lane and E Campbell, *Dunadd: an early Dalriadic capital*, Cardiff Studies in Archaeology, Oxbow Books, 201-212

Bayliss, A, Hines, J, and Høilund Nielsen, K, 2013 Interpretive chronologies for the female graves, in A Bayliss, J, Hines, K, Høilund Nielsen, G, McCormac and C Scull, *Anglo-Saxon graves and grave goods of the 6th and 7th centuries AD: a chronological framework,* Society for Medieval Archaeology Monograph, **33**, 339-458

Bender Jørgensen, L, 1986 *Forhistoriske textiler i Skandinavien: Prehistoric Scandinavian Textiles*, Nordiske Fortidsminder Series B, **9**, Copenhagen

Bender Jørgensen, L, 1992 North *European textiles until AD 1000*, Aarhus

Biddle, M, 1990 *Object and economy in medieval Winchester: Artefacts from medieval Winchester*, Winchester Studies, **7**.ii

Bimson, M, and Oddy, W A, 1983 Bronze alloys in Dark Age Europe, in R Bruce -Mitford, *The Sutton Hoo ship-burial*, **3.1**, British Museum, 945-961

Bone, P, 1989 The Development of Anglo-Saxon swords from the Fifth to the Eleventh Century, in S Hawkes (ed), *Weapons and warfare in Anglo-Saxon England*, Oxford University Committee for Archaeology, **21**, 63-70

Brenan, J, 1991 *Hanging bowls and their contexts; and archaeological survey of their socio-economic significance from the fifth to seventh centuries AD*, British Archaeological Reports, British Series, **220**

Brodribb, A C C, Hands, A R, and Walker, D R, 1973 *Excavations at Shakenoak Farm, near Wilcote, Oxfordshire, part IV: site C,* (Roman structures and Saxon burial ground), Private publication

Brothwell, D, 1972 *Digging up Bone*, (2nd edition), British Museum (Natural History), London

Brown, A E, and Foard, G, 2004 The Anglo-Saxon period, in M Tingle (ed), *The Archaeology of Northamptonshire*, Northamptonshire Archaeological Society, 78-101

Brown, A E, Key, T R, and Orr, C, 1977 Some Anglo-Saxon estates and their boundaries in South-West Nothamptonshire, *Northamptonshire Archaeology*, **12**, 155-176

Brown, A E, Key, T R, Orr, C, and Woodfield, P, 1981 The Stowe charter – a revision and some implications, *Northamptonshire Archaeology*, **16**, 136-147

Brown, A G, and Meadows, I D, Turner, S D, and Mattingly, D J, 2001 Roman vineyards in Britain: stratigraphic and palynological data from Wollaston in the Nene Valley, England, *Antiquity*, **75** issue 290, 745-757

Brown, J, forthcoming *Archaeology and highway development in Central Bedfordshire: The M1 Junction 12 improvements and the A5-M1 link road*, MOLA monograph

Bruce-Mitford, R L S, 1972 *The Sutton Hoo Ship-burial*, British Museum Press (second edition)

Bruce-Mitford, R L S, 1974 *Aspects of Anglo-Saxon archaeology: Sutton Hoo and other discoveries*, London

Bushe-Fox, J P, 1926 *First report on the excavations of a Roman fort at Richborough, Kent* Society of Antiquaries Research Report, **16**

Caley, E, 1964 *Orichalcum and related ancient alloys: origin, composition, and manufacture, with special reference to the coinage of the Roman Empire*, Numismatic Notes and Mongraphs, **151**, New York, American Numismatic Society

Cameron, E A, 2000 *Sheaths and scabbards in England AD400-1000*, British Archaeological Reports British Series, **301**

Caple, C, forthcoming The Yarm helmet, submitted to *Medieval Archaeology*

Carver, M O H, 1998 *Sutton Hoo: Burial ground of Kings?*, British Museum Press

Carroll, J, 1995 Millefiori in the development of Early Irish Metalworking in C Bourke (ed), *From the Isles of the North, Early Medieval Art in Britain and Ireland,* 49-57

Chapman, A, 1997, The excavation of Neolithic and medieval mounds at Tansor Crossroads, *Northamptonshire Archaeology*, **27**, 3-50

Chapman, A, 2001 Excavation of an Iron Age Settlement and a Middle Saxon Cemetery at Great Houghton, Northampton 1996, *Northamptonshire Archaeology,* **29**, 1-41

Chapman, A, forthcoming The Radiocarbon dates, in J H Williams, M Shaw and A Chapman, Anglo-Saxon Northampton, *Northamptonshire Archaeology*

Chapman, A, and Jackson, D, 1992 Wollaston Bypass, Northamptonshire, salvage excavations 1984, *Northamptonshire Archaeology*, **24**, 67-75

Church, A J, and Brodribb, W J, 1868 *The Agricola and Germany of Tacitus,* translated into English by A J Church and W J Brodribb

Cooper, N, 2000 *The archaeology of Rutland Water*, Leicester Archaeology Monograph, **6**

Courtney, P, 1981 The Early Saxon Fenland A Reconsideration, in D Brown, J Campbell and S Chadwick Hawkes (eds), *Anglo-Saxon Studies in Archaeology and History 2*, British Archaeological Reports, British Series, **92**, 91-99

Craddock, P T, 2001 Conservative metal alloying traditions in the migration period, *Acta Metallurgica Slovaca*, **7**, 175-181

Crowfoot, E, 1988 Textiles: *Wakerley, Northants, Anglo-Saxon cemetery*, Ancient Monuments Laboratory Report, **88/44**

Dark, K, 2000 *Britain and the End of the Roman Empire*, Tempus

Davies, S, 2004 *Welsh military institutions, 633-1283*, Cardiff

Davies, W, and Vierck, H, 1974 The contexts of the Tribal Hidage: social aggregates and settlement patterns, *Frühmittelalterlice Stűdien*, **8**, 223-93

Dickinson, T, 1973 Bronze objects, in A C C Broadribb et al, Excavations at Shakenoak Farm, Part IV, Site C, (Roman structures and Saxon burial ground), Private publication, 116-7

Drinkall, G, and Foreman, M, 1998 *The Anglo-Saxon cemetery at Castledyke South, Barton-on-Humber*, Sheffield

Eremin, K, Graham-Campbell, J, and Wilthew, P, 2002 Analysis of copper alloy artefacts from pagan Norse graves in Scotland, *Archaeometry*, **98**

Everson, P, 1993 Pre-Viking settlement in Lindsey, in A Vince (ed), *Pre-Viking Lindsey*, Lincoln, Lincoln Archaeological Studies, **1**, 91–100

Evison, V I, 1988 *An Anglo-Saxon cemetery at Alton, Hampshire*, Hampshire Field Club Archaeological Society Monograph, **4**

Evison, V I, 1994 *An Anglo-Saxon cemetery at Great Chesterford, Essex,* Council for British Archaeology Research Report, **91**

Fern, C, Dickinson, T, and Webster, L (eds), in prep *The Staffordshire Hoard: an Anglo-Saxon Treasure*, Society of Antiquaries of London

Filmer-Sankey, W, and Pestell, T, 2001 *Snape Anglo-Saxon Cemetery: excavation and surveys 1824-1992*, East Anglian Archaeology, **95**, Ipswich

Farley, M, 2010 Saxon Buckinghamshire (AD410-1066), in M Farley (ed), *An illustrated History of Early Buckinghamshire*, Buckinghamshire Archaeological Society, 109-150

Foard, G, 1985 The administrative organisation of Northamptonshire in the Saxon Period, *Anglo-Saxon Studies in Archaeology*, **4**, 185-222

Foard, G, 1999 An Archaeological Resource Assessment of Anglo-Saxon Northamptonshire (400 - 1066) https://www2.le.ac.uk/services/.../the-east-midlands-archaeological-research-framework accessed 12th June 2018

Fordham, H G, 1904 A small bronze object found near Guilden Morden, *Proceedings of the Cambridgeshire Antiquarian Society*, **10.4**, 373-374

Foster, J, 1977 A boar figurine from Guilden Morden, Cambs, *Medieval Archaeology*, **21**, 166-167

Frank, R, 2008 *The boar on the helmet, in C E Karkov and E Damico Aedificia Nova: studies in honour of Rosemary Cramp*, Western Michigan University, 76–88

Gage, J, 1834 *A plan of barrows called the Bartlow Hill, in the parish of Ashdon, Essex, with an account of Roman sepulchral relics recently discovered in the lesser barrow,* Archaeologia, **25**, 1-23

Geake, H, 1997 *The use of grave-goods in conversion period England*, British Archaeological Reports, British Series, **261**

Geake, H, 1999a When were hanging bowls deposited in Anglo-Saxon Graves?, *Medieval Archaeology*, **43**, 1-18

Geake, H, 1999b Invisible kingdoms: the use of grave-goods in seventh-century England, *Anglo-Saxon Studies in Archaeology and History*, **10**, 203-215

Geake, H, 2003 The Control of Burial Practice in middle Anglo-Saxon England, in M Carver (ed), *The Cross Goes North: Processes of Conversion in Northern Europe, AD 300-1300,* Boydell, 259-270

Gibson, A N, and McCormick, A, 1985 Archaeology at Grendon Quarry, Northamptonshire. Part 1: Neolithic and Bronze Age sites excavated in 1974-5, *Northamptonshire Archaeology*, **20**, 23-66

Gover, J E B, Allen, M, and Stenton, F M, 1975 *The place-names of Northamptonshire*, English Place-Name Society, **10**

Gravett, C, 1992 *Hastings 1066: the fall of Saxon England*, Osprey Publishing

Grinsell, L V, 1991 Barrows in Anglo-Saxon land charters, The Antiquaries Journal, **LXXI**, 46-63

Hadley, D M, 2001 *Death in medieval England*, Tempus

Hall, D, 1977 *Wollaston: portrait of a village*, The Wollaston Society

Hall, D, 1995 *The open fields of Northamptonshire*, Northamptonshire Record Society, **XXXVIII**

Hardy, A, Charles, B M, and Williams, R J, 2007 *Death and taxes: the archaeology of a middle Saxon estate centre at Higham Ferrers, Northamptonshire*, Oxford Archaeology

Härke, H, 1989 Knives in early Saxon burials: blade length and age at death, *Medieval Archaeology*, **33**, 144-48, Oxford Academic

Härke, H, 1990 Warrior graves? The background of the Anglo-Saxon weapon burial rite, *Past and Present*, **126**, 22-43

Härke, H, 1992 Changing symbols in a changing society: the Anglo-Saxon weapon burial rite in the seventh century, in M Carver (ed), *The Age of Sutton Hoo*, Woodbridge, 149-166

Härke, H, 1997 Material culture as myth: weapons in Anglo-Saxon graves, in C K Jensen and K Høilund Nielsen (eds), *burial and society*, Aarhus University Press, 119-27

Hart, C R, 1977 The Kingdom of Mercia, in A Dornier, *Mercian Studies*, 43-61

Hassall, M, and Rhodes, J, 1974 Excavations at the new Market Hall, Gloucester, 1966-7, *Transactions of Bristol and Gloucester Archaeological Society,* **42**, 15-100

Heaney, S, 2000 *Beowulf: a new verse translation*, New York

Hirst, S M, 1985 *An Anglo-Saxon inhumation cemetery at Sewerby, East Yorkshire*, York University Archaeology Publication, **4**

Hood, J, Ager, B, Williams, C, Harrington, S, and Cartwright, C, 2012 Investigating and interpreting an early-to-mid sixth-century Frankish style helmet, *The British museum technical research bulletin*, **6**, 83-95

Hundt, H-J, 1966 Die textilien aus den Gräbern, in R Christlein, *Das Alamannische Reihengräberfeld von Marktoberdorf in Allgäu*, 93-102

Hundt, H-J, 1972 Die Textilien aus dem Reihengräberfriedhof von Donzdorf, in E M Neuffer, *Der Reihengräberfriedhof von Donzdorf'*, Forschungen und Berichte zur Vor-und Frühgeschichichte in Baden-Württemberg, **2**, 97-108

Hundt, H-J, 1978 Die Textilreste, in, P Paulsen and H Schach-Dörges, 149-163

Hunt, J, 2016 *Warriors, warlords and saints: the Anglo-Saxon kingdom of Mercia*, West Midlands History

Hyslop, M, 1963 Two Anglo-Saxon cemeteries at Chamberlains Barn, Leighton Buzzard, Bedfordshire, *Archaeological Journal,* **120**, 161-200

Jackson, D, nd *An archaeological evaluation at Wollaston*, Northamptonshire Archaeology report

Jackson, D, 1991 An archaeological evaluation at Wollaston, *Northamptonshire Archaeology*, **23**, 83-85

Jackson, D, 1995 Archaeology at Grendon Quarry, Northamptonshire. Part 2: Other prehistoric, Iron Age and later sites excavated in 1974-75 and further observations between 1976-80, *Northamptonshire Archaeology*, **26**, 3-32

Jones, G, 1968 *The history of the Vikings, Appendix 3*, 425-30, Oxford University Press

Jones, H, 1997 *The Region of Derbyshire and North Staffordshire from AD350 to AD700: an analysis of Romano-British and Anglian barrow use in the White Peak*, Unpublished Ph.D. thesis, University of Nottingham

Jones, R, and Page, M, 2006 *Medieval villages in an English landscape: beginnings and ends*, Windgather Press

Kendrick, T D, 1932 British Hanging Bowls *Antiquity,* **6**, 161-84

Kidd, A M, 1994 *Proposed extension to Earls Barton Quarry, Hardwater Road, Wollaston, Northants: Archaeological Evaluation Brief*, Northamptonshire County Council

Kidd, A M, 1995 *Land south of Hardwater Road, Wollaston, Northamptonshire, Planning Application WP/94/439c: Archaeological Recording Action Brief*, Northamptonshire County Council

Laing, L, 1993 *A catalogue of Celtic ornamental metalwork in the British Isles cAD400-1200,* British Archaeological Reports, British Series, **229**

Laing, L, 1999 The Bradwell mount and the use of millefiori in post-Roman Britain, *Studia Celtica,* **33**, 137-53

Lang, J, and Ager, B, 1989 Swords of the Anglo-Saxon and Viking periods in the British Museum: a Radiographic study in S Hawkes (ed) *Weapons and warfare in Anglo-Saxon England*, 85-122, Oxford University Committee for Archaeology Monograph, **21**

Lucy, S, 2000 *The Anglo-Saxon way of death*, Sutton

Malim, T, and Hines, J, 1998 *The Anglo-Saxon Cemetery at Edix Hill (Barrington A), Cambridgeshire,* Council for British Archaeology Research Report, **112**

Marzinzik, S, 2003 *Early Anglo-Saxon Belt Buckles (late 5th to early 8th centuries A.D.). Their classification and context*, British Archaeological Report, British Series, **357**

Meadows, I D, 1994 Wollaston; Pioneer Aggregates Quarry, *South Midlands Archaeology*, **24**, 23-24

Meadows, I D, 1995 *Land south of Hardwater Road, Wollaston, Northants. Archaeological evaluation: stage 1 (assessment)*, Northamptonshire Archaeology report

Meadows, I D, 1997 The Pioneer Helmet, *Northamptonshire Archaeology,* **27**, 191-193

Meadows, I D, 1997 Wollaston: the 'Pioneer' helmet, *Current Archaeology*, **154**, 391-5

Meadows, I D, 2004 *An Anglian burial from Wollaston, Northamptonshire,* Northamptonshire Archaeology report

Meadows, I D, and Atkins, R, forthcoming Excavation of a prehistoric and Roman landscape at Wollaston, *Northamptonshire Archaeology*

Meaney, A, 2003 Anglo-Saxon Pagan and Early Christian Attitude to the Dead, in M Carver (ed), *The Cross Goes North: Processes of Conversion in Northern Europe, AD 300-1300,* Boydell, 229-242

Metcalf, D M, 1977 Monetary affairs in Mercia in the time of Aethelbald (716-57), in A Dornier (ed), *Mercian Studies*, Leicester University Press, 87-106

Morillo, S, 1994 *Warfare under the Anglo-Norman Kings, 1066-1135*, Boydell and Brewer Ltd

Mortimer, C, Pollard A M, and Scull, C, 1986 XRF analyses of some Anglo-Saxon copper– alloy finds from Watchfield, Oxfordshire, *Historical Metallurgy*, **20.1**, 36-42

Mortimer, R, 2000 Village development and ceramic sequence: the Middle to Late Saxon village at Lordship Lane, Cottenham, Cambridgeshire, *Proceedings of the Cambridge Antiquarian Society*, **89**, 5-33

Muldowney, M, 2013 *Archaeological Mitigation Works at The Coach House, Middleton Cheney, Northamptonshire*, Northamptonshire Archaeology report, **13/232**

Northover, J P, 1991 Further comments on the composition of the Breiddin bronzes, in C R Musson, *The Breidden Hillfort*, Council for British Archaeology Research Report, **76**, 210-18

O'Brien, E, 1999 *Post-Roman Britain to Anglo-Saxon England: burial practices reviewed*, British Archaeological Report, British Series, **289**

Oddy, W A, Bimson, M, and Cowell, M C, 1983 'Scientific examination of the Sutton-Hoo hanging–bowls (appendix B) in R Bruce-Mitford, *The Sutton Hoo ship burial*, **3.1**, 299-315

Ozanne, A, 1962–3 The Peak Dwellers, *Medieval Archaeology*, **6–7**, 15–52

Parry, S, and Audouy, M, 1995 *Land south of Hardwater Road, Wollaston, Northants. Archaeological evaluation: stage 2 (geophysical survey and sample excavation)*, Northamptonshire Archaeology report

Paulsen, P, and Schach-Dörges, H, 1978 *Das alamannische Gräberfeld von Geingen an der Brenz*, Stuttgart

Penhallurick, R D, 1986 *Tin in Antiquity*, The Institute of Metals, London

Ponting, M J, 1999 East meets west in post-Classical Bet She'an: the archaeolometallurgy of culture change, *Journal of Archaeological Science*, **26**, 1311-1321

RCHM(E), 1979 *An Inventory of the Historical Monuments in the County of Northampton; 2: Archaeological Sites in Central Northamptonshire*, Royal Commission on Historical Monuments (England)

Samuels, J, and Russell, A, 1999 An Anglo-Saxon Burial near Winthorpe Road, Newark, Nottinghamshire, *Transactions of the Thoroton Society*, **103**, 57–83

Semmelmann, K, and Ashworth, H, 2004 *Land at Dando Close, Wollaston, Northants, Archaeological Assessment Report*, Heritage Network report, **205**

Sherley-Price, L, (translation) 1968 Bede, Historia ecclesiastica Gentis Anglorum, Book III

Shipley, A, and Finn, C, 2018 *Archaeological mitigation on land east of Warwick Road, Kibworth Harcourt, Leicestershire, November 2017 to December 2017*, MOLA Northampton report, **18/62**

Simmonds, C, 2017 *Archaeological Excavation on land at Pineham, Zone H Northamptonshire September 2015 to May 2016: Assessment Report and Updated Project Design*, MOLA report, **17/29**

Speake, G, 1989 *A Saxon Bed –burial on Swallowcliffe Down*, English Heritage Archaeology Report, **10**

Spoerry, P, and Atkins, R, 2015 *A late Saxon village and medieval manor: excavations at Botolph Bridge, Orton Longueville, Peterborough*, East Anglian Archaeology, **153**

Swanton, M, 1996 *The Anglo-Saxon Chronicle*, Orion

Taylor, C, and Angus, C, *1999 Peterborough to Lutton 1050mm gas pipeline, archaeological evaluation, excavation and watching brief 1998* (two volumes), Network Archaeological report, **135**

Tweddle, D, 1992 The *Anglian Helmet from Coppergate*, Archaeology of York Fascicule, **17/8**

Unglik, H, 1991 Structure, composition and technology of late Roman copper alloy artefacts from the Canadian excavations at Carthage, *Archaeomaterials*, **5**, 91-110

Upson-Smith, T, 2000 *Saxon burial at Whitehall Farm, Nether Heyford, Northamptonshire*, Northamptonshire Archaeology report, **2686**

Upson-Smith, T, 2016 A middle to late Saxon cemetery at Rothley, The Grange, *Leicestershire Archaeological and Historical Society*, **90**, 103-139

Vince, A, 2006 The Anglo-Saxon Period (cAD400–850), in N J Cooper (ed), *the archaeology of the East Midlands: An Archaeological Resource Assessment and Research Agenda*, Leicester Archaeology Monographs, **13**, 161-184

Walton-Rogers, P, 2006 Textile and clothing, in P Williams and R Newman, *Market Lavington, Wiltshire: Anglo-Saxon Cemetery and Settlement - Excavations at Grove Farm, 1986-90*, Wessex Archaeology monograph

Watson, J, and Edwards, G, 1990 Conservation of material from Anglo-Saxon cemeteries, in E Southworth (ed), *Anglo-Saxon cemeteries: a reappraisal*, Sutton, 97-106

Webster, L, 1992 Death's diplomacy: Sutton Hoo in the light of other male princely burials, in R Farrell and C Newman de Vegvar (eds), *Sutton Hoo: fifty years after*, Oxbow Books, 75-82

Webster, L, and Backhouse, J (ed) 1991 *The making of England, Anglo-Saxon art and culture AD600-900*, British Museum Press

West, S E, 1988 *The Anglo-Saxon cemetery at Westgarth Gardens, Bury St Edmunds, Suffolk*, East Anglian Archaeological Report, **38**

Williams, H, 1999 Placing the dead: investigating the location of wealthy barrow burials in the seventh century, in M Rundkvist (ed), *Grave matters: eight studies of burial data from the first millennium AD from Crimea, Scandinavia and England*, British Archaeological Reports, International Series, **781**, 57-86

Williams, H, 2006 *Death and memory in early medieval Britain*, Cambridge University Press

Williams, H, 2010 Engendered bodies and objects of memory in final phase graves, in J Buckberry and A Cherryson (eds), *Burial in the later Anglo-Saxon England c.650-1100AD*, Oxbow Books, 26-37

Wills, J, 2014 *The Wollaston burial: a grave's political and religious place in the landscape,* http://www.academia.edu/7818149/The_Wollaston_Burial_A_Grave_s_Political_and_Religious_Place_in_the_Landscape, *accessed 13th August 2018*

Youngs, S, 1998 Medieval hanging bowls from Wiltshire, *Wiltshire Archaeological and Natural History Magazine,* **91**, 35-41

Yorke, B, 1990 *Kings and kingdoms of early Anglo-Saxon England*, London